PM&R Oral Boards
Made Easy
40 Oral Board Practice Cases

PM&R Prep Pros
2nd Edition

Copyright © 2022 PM&R Prep Pros

All rights reserved.

ISBN-13: 9780578390680
ISBN-10: 057839068X

DEDICATION

To our families who put us through medical school, residency, the early years of our career, and who were also with us through the ups and downs, thick and thin - we would not be where we are or who we are without them. Also, we dedicate this to our mentors and teachers who gave us strong foundations to expand our knowledge.

Table of Contents

Disclaimer 1
Approach And Strategies 2
Warm Up Cases 12
Advanced Cases 108
Afterword 196
About The Authors 197

DISCLAIMER

This book does not guarantee board score and certification. It is not intended to be used to diagnose and/or treat medical conditions, nor should it be used as such. The authors and editors are not responsible for any errors or omissions within this book. The practice cases are the products of the author's imagination. Any similarity between these practice cases and resemblance to actual persons, living or dead, or actual events is purely coincidental. Medicine is constantly changing and the content within this book should be viewed within this light. This is a text of practice cases to prepare for an oral examination, not for clinical diagnosis and treatment.

APPROACH AND STRATEGIES

Welcome! You have likely spent enormous sums of money on medical school, sacrificed countless hours of sleepless nights during residency, and poured forth even more resources to finally be eligible for the Oral Boards - the last step before achieving Board Certification as a Physiatrist. Congratulations! It is time to put all of that effort into passing this final test and to avoid making the trip to Mayo Clinic in Rochester more than once.

This book is intended to be used as a study guide for the deliberate practice and actionable approach to preparing for the ABPM&R Oral Boards. The vignettes in this book are not the key to passing the test. Rather, the key to passing any test is to understand what the examiner (in this case the ABPM&R) is testing and quantifying. This book offers structured studying and deliberate practice to help guide you in practicing for the Oral Boards. Consider this text a supplement to your primary study resources, not a replacement.

General Guidelines

1. Practice, practice, practice - recognize discrete question types and what is being tested with a study partner.
2. Recommend broad interventions and workup. There may not be cost associations or limited resources that you are used to dealing with in your actual practice setting.
3. Have multiple differential diagnosis and work through them. List all tests that work up the

differential diagnosis. Your fund of knowledge, not just your ability to nail a particular diagnosis, is key.

4. When answering questions regarding communication and interpersonal skills, focus on empathy and willingness to partner with the person to ensure the best possible outcome. Role-play to practice these skills at length with a study partner.

Virtual Examination Format

1. Remember to review all content on the ABPM&R website regarding the virtual format. As this format is relatively new there may be considerable changes from exam to exam.

2. Read the ABPM&R guidance for preparation of your testing area and prepare your area at least one day in advance.

3. The dress code has not changed in the virtual examination format: dress in business professional clothing.

4. Test your equipment (computer, microphone, headphones, internet connection). Consider practicing with your partner using the equipment and setting that you will be testing with to minimize potential technical difficulties. Consider using your cellphone mobile hotspot tethering as a backup connection.

5. If you feel you are getting bogged down in one section, consider pausing or taking a sip of water to see if your examiner moves you on.

Travel (If exam returns to in-person format)

1. Flights: Plan your visit to Rochester, Minnesota, well ahead of the exam. Allot time for extended travel and the possibility of inclement weather. There are two options for airports - Minneapolis-St. Paul (approximately 80 miles from Rochester) and Rochester (a smaller airport). There are many hotels within walking distance to Mayo Clinic. Weather may be unpredictable in May, so plan to get to Rochester at least 24 hours in advance.

2. Ground Transportation: If flying into the Minneapolis-St. Paul airport, consider using a shuttle service to get your hotel in Rochester.

3. Dining: There are a variety of restaurants and cafes located within a short walk from the testing site. There is a food court in the shopping center nearby for a quick bite and multiple coffee shops in the area to study and reconnect with colleagues.

4. Dress Code: Dress appropriately for the examination. Your dress should be business professional.

5. Review the ABPM&R's videos of the examination setting and sample cases (Example Vignettes). These are invaluable in preparing for the format of the test.

Approach to Answering Each Practice Case

Familiarize yourself with a standardized approach to addressing the practice cases. The practice cases are divided up into discrete question types. Recognize what type of question each section represents and answer accordingly. We propose a standardized approach below, but deliberate practice of a standardized approach means fine tuning and tailoring your approach to your needs with every practice session.

Cases in this text are separated into two sections: Warm Up Cases and Advanced Cases. They both follow the same general format, as noted below. Use the Warm Up Cases to familiarize yourself with a standardized approach to practice cases. Then move on to the Advanced Cases to expand your differential diagnoses and for additional rehabilitation topics to review.

Question types to recognize:

I. **Data Acquisition Questions**
    A. FAR COLDER - Go back to your medical student days. Start with the basic elements of history. Ask about **F**requency, **A**ssociating symptoms, **R**adiation, **C**haracteristic, **O**nset, **L**ocation, **D**uration, **E**xacerbating circumstances, and **R**elieving factors.
    B. Focused history - During the FAR COLDER history taking with your examiner, you should have jotted down your top 5 differential diagnosis. Now ask focused history questions for each of the 5 differential diagnosis you have written down.
    C. Systems based physical Examination - The examiner will move you on to the physical examination portion of the test. The approach is similar to history taking - take the physical examination like a medical student. Ask an exhaustive, multiple system, physical examination including orientation, HEENT, CV, lungs, abdominal exam, detailed

neurologic examination, and **specialty examinations**.
D. Focused physical examination - Based on your top 5 differential diagnosis, ask for focused physical examination results.

II. **Problem Solving Questions**
A. These questions ask you to go through your differential diagnosis. It is helpful to verbalize the history and exam findings that support each differential diagnosis.

III. **Patient Management Questions**
A. Tests - Broadly ask for tests to work up your top 5 differential diagnosis, starting with the most reasonable ones. Verbalize why you are ordering each test. This includes x-rays, labs, MRI's, biopsies, EMG's, CSF, urine analysis, etc.
B. Medical management - After the tests portion, your practice questioner may tell you what the diagnosis is. Do not get **hung up** on the case if you have missed the diagnosis. Move forward as now you will need to medically manage the patient. The management should be a team based approach. Envision an inpatient rehabilitation services and what each member of the team would provide your patient. That is how you should approach this question.
   1. Physician - What medications would this patient need? Are there other specialty referrals that are also needed?
   2. Nurse - What bowel, bladder, or wound care needs are there?

3. Speech - Does this patient need speech therapy?
4. PT - Does this patient need physical therapy? What are the associated equipment needs?
5. OT - Does this patient need occupational therapy? What the associated equipment needs?
6. SPL – Does this patient need speech therapy? Are there cognitive deficits, visual changes, swallowing difficulties, etc.?
7. Neuropsychology - Are there any neuropsychological issues or educational needs?
8. Social work - What are the social issues affecting this patient?
9. Community resources - Would these be helpful for the patient?
10. Discharge planning - What other miscellaneous issues must be addressed for comprehensive treatment of this patient?

IV. Systems based practice questions
    A. This practice question may be presented when the patient is transitioned to inpatient rehabilitation or follows up for outpatient rehabilitation. You should approach the question the same way as medical management and go through a team based approach.

V. **Interpersonal and communication skills questions**
    A. This is your chance to shine as an exceptionally empathetic, caring physician. While it is recommended to practice all cases out loud, *this* question is essential to practice verbally, ideally with a study partner who challenges you during role playing.
    B. **NURSE** - Answer this question using the acronym NURSE.
        1. **N**ame the emotion that the patient or family member(s) is displaying.
        2. State you want more information because you want to **U**nderstand what the patient is going through.
        3. After the examiner gives you more information, state that you **R**espect what the patient is going through.
        4. **S**ympathize with the patient by stating that what they are going through must be extremely difficult.
        5. **E**mpathize with the patient by stating that you would feel the same way in their shoes and that you are on their team. Also, let them know that you will continue to with them towards recovery by bringing them back in frequently, advocating on their behalf, connecting them with community resources, and so on.

Approach to Study Topics & Making Your Own Questions

Remember, this is just a small selection of practice cases. Creating your own questions to quiz yourself and your study partners is encouraged to allow mastery of the process. This approach to studying should be used for making questions under each class.

Go to the ABPM&R Part II Examination Outline. Study one topic at a time under each major class of "Patient Diagnosis". With the first cycle, study the most commonly presenting topic under that class. For example, under "Class A Cerebral Vascular Accidents," you would most likely study "1. Embolic/Thrombotic." You would then move on to "Class B Central Nervous System" and study the subcategory there that is the most commonly presenting diagnosis. After the first cycle, move in to the second cycle and find the second most commonly presenting diagnosis under that class. Proceed in this manner from Class A to I.

This approach ensures 3 things:

1. You will study the high-yield topics for the examination.
2. You will have multiple exposures to the same class of diagnosis, and often times differentials and study material will overlap and give you repetition.
3. You will work towards more esoteric diagnosis and broaden your own knowledge.

Other Thoughts and Considerations

Deliberate Practice is key.

- Deliberate Practice means **consistency** every week. You MUST set aside time every week to practice, preferably daily. Adopt the mindset of an athlete training to compete in an upcoming event. Start your deliberate practice at a minimum of 3-4 months before the test.

- Have a study partner to keep you **accountable**. Accountability will mean you will practice no matter what, even when you are feeling overwhelmed and overworked in your position as a new attending or fellow.

- Practice **out loud**. This is an oral examination. Deliberate practice means practicing in the mode of the examination which is oral.

- Write questions and have you and your study partner **test** each other. Writing the questions makes you think like your examiner. It makes you focus in on the relevant diagnostic information. Testing each other makes you realize what your examiner is looking for, so when it is your turn to answer you know how to respond to your examiner.

With deliberate practice using the same mode and focused thought pattern, your brain will naturally kick into the neurologic pathways you reinforced every week. Like any skilled athlete, you will not need to strain your brain and will reflexively kick into test mode.

Keep your body healthy. This is a 3-hour test with multiple questions to answer. In the case of an in person examination, you will have to fly in and possibly transfer multiple times to get to Rochester. There may be snowstorms, so arrive early (even 24 hours ahead of time is not unreasonable). You will be physically fatigued. Stay hydrated. Exercise often. Eat well. If your body does not function optimally, your brain will also not function optimally.

WARM UP CASES

A. Hip Pain
B. Hand Pain
C. Parkinson's Disease
D. Mixed Weakness
E. Burn Injury
F. Leg Weakness
G. Dizziness
H. Back Pain
I. Cerebral Palsy
J. Knee Pain
K. Shoulder Pain
L. Hip Crepitation
M. Elbow Pain
N. Heel Pain
O. Hip Pain
P. Chest Pain
Q. Multiple Sclerosis
R. Hip Pain
S. Cardiac Rehabilitation
T. Hand weakness
U. Heel Pain
V. Deconditioning

W. Pelvic Pain

X. Stroke

Y. Neck Pain

Case: Hip pain

1. A 68-years-old male presents to your outpatient rehabilitation clinic reporting right hip pain. What information would you like to know?

2. Symptoms started 2 months ago, insidious onset, with aching pain over the right lateral hip, worse with sleeping on his right side, relieved with oral Ibuprofen, non-radiating, gradually worsening. There is no significant prior medical history aside from obesity, and he denies any substance use. He had recently changed his level of activity by trying to lose weight through jogging. What would you like to ascertain on a focused physical examination?

3. He has an increased abdominal girth and ambulates with a slight antalgic gait (favoring his right side). He is tender to palpation just posterior to the right greater trochanter, reproducing his pain, as well as tender along the right iliotibial band. Patrick's test and resisted hip abduction is painful at the lateral hip. Ober's test is positive. Stinchfield, hip scour and straight leg raise are negative. He has bilateral pes planus, worse with weight bearing. What is your diagnosis and your rehabilitation prescription for his pain? Is any imaging warranted?

4. The patient has greater trochanter pain syndrome, a relatively common cause of lateral hip pain. Education on gait mechanics, arch supports, relative rest from aggravating exercise with a gradual return to aerobic exercise is recommended. Additionally, a course of physical therapy to address glute activation, ITB stretches, jogging form, and developing a home exercise program would be ideal. A local corticosteroid injection may be considered, as may oral or topical analgesics; although a

recent controlled trial noted education and exercise resulted in better outcomes than a steroid injection alone. A right hip x-ray may be considered to rule out underlying fracture. If there was a clinical history suggestive of trauma and risk factors for avascular necrosis, further imaging such as MRA of the hip would be warranted.

Two weeks later, after just starting physical therapy, the patient calls your office. He is frustrated by his condition and at this time he doesn't seem to have had a major improvement in symptoms. He reports seeing an advertisement for a new "laser" treatment for hip pain, and wonders if you would recommend this for treating his condition instead ?

5. Listen to his concerns and express empathy regarding his situation and frustration. This condition is often self-limiting, but can persist for up to 1-2 years. Then offer information on laser treatments as a modality. They are often used in therapy environments to help address musculoskeletal injuries. However, they should not be expected in isolation to resolve greater trochanteric pain syndrome. Instead, a multi-faceted approach with medications, targeted exercise program, and activity modification are necessary and will likely yield the best results. You may offer to request his physical therapist trial laser as a modality during therapy sessions, but not as the sole treatment, nor should it be the focus of each therapy session. Be sure to note your plan for follow up with your clinic during his therapy course to ensure the best outcome and that you will continue to address his concerns as needed.

1 month later, the patient returns, reporting significant benefit with PT. His therapist recommended several additional sessions to finalize his home exercise program.

However, his health insurance refuses to cover future therapy sessions. How would you handle this?

6. Start by reviewing the documentation of progress with therapy and identifying where further sessions may be warranted. From this, you should offer to advocate for additional sessions with his health insurance if appropriate, describing the likely benefits of such therapy in helping prevent further recurrence of this condition. If they still will not cover further visits, you may bring the patient back to your clinic and review additional therapeutic exercises with him. Additionally, he could pay out of pocket for one or two extra sessions, requesting a focus on completion of his home exercise program with the therapist in light of his financial constraints.

Notes: The term "trochanteric bursitis" has slowly gone out of favor, in part due to the recognition of the multifactorial nature of this syndrome. It is now more commonly referred to as greater trochanteric pain syndrome, a more all-encompassing term that includes the gluteal tendinopathies often involved rather than just bursitis. Mainstays of treatment include activity modification, focused skilled therapy for stretching and strengthening, and with local corticosteroid injection potentially beneficial as well.

References:

Reid, D. (2016). The management of greater trochanteric pain syndrome: A systematic literature review. *Journal of Orthopaedics, 13*(1), 15-28. doi:10.1016/j.jor.2015.12.006

Mellor, R. et al. (2018). Education plus exercise versus corticosteroid injection use versus a wait and see approach on global outcome and pain from gluteal tendinopathy: prospective, single blinded, randomized clinical trial. *BMJ* 2018; 361 :k1662

Case: Hand Pain

A 29-years-old male mechanic presents to your outpatient rehabilitation clinic reporting right-sided hand pain.

1. What would you like to find out on history and physical examination to better determine the etiology of the hand pain?

2. Hand pain has been present intermittently for the last 1 year without an inciting event, is described as a heavy, aching sensation in his dominant right hand (he believes all digits are involved, but is not entirely sure), is worse after riding his bike, and does not seem to involve any weakness. It often wakes him up at night and is relieved by shaking his hand vigorously. He denies any prior medical history or surgical history. His physical examination is noted for mild right thenar eminence atrophy, positive right median nerve compression, and Tinel's sign at the wrist. Reflexes and strength are within normal limits, except for trace abductor pollicis brevis weakness on right and diminished sensation over digits 1-3. Finkelstein's, Adson's, Spurling's, Tinel's at the elbow are all negative. What is your differential diagnosis for the cause of his hand pain? What, if any, further workup would be warranted?

3. X-rays of his hand and wrist are unremarkable. His electrodiagnostic study returns, demonstrating right-sided increased median sensory distal latency with delayed motor responses that also have diminished amplitude. Ulnar and radial responses are within normal limits. The needle examination of the first dorsal interosseous and pronator teres are within normal limits. However, the abductor pollicis brevis has trace fibrillations on spontaneous activity assessment and slightly reduced recruitment. He would like

to avoid surgery at all costs. What is your rehabilitation plan?

4. You offer counseling regarding his likely diagnosis of carpal tunnel syndrome and education on potential etiologies. You also offer a surgical referral given his weakness and findings on EMG, but the patient declines. You order a course of Occupational Therapy (for nerve flossing exercises, nighttime wrist splints, myofascial release, scapular stabilization, and modalities). Education on activity modification and ergonomics at work may be helpful. Additionally, you offer a course of topical or oral analgesics to help with the symptoms. The patient asks you, "Doc, I'm scared, exactly how bad is this? Could it get worse?"

5. Utilizing lay terms, start with offering reassurance and empathy for his condition, and explain what CTS is. CTS is a common nerve condition and many people may improve by changing their activity and other conservative management options. However, while you respect his wishes to avoid seeing a surgeon, note the weakness and nerve study findings point to worsening, advanced CTS, with the potential for continued weakness that might limit his ability to work. Ensure close follow up to revisit the question of hand surgery referral, and offer to continue to work with him to ensure the best possible outcome.

Notes:

1. Attempt to characterize the hand pain. Is it isolated to the hand or radiating? What parts of the hand are involved? What is the nature of the pain? What are aggravating and alleviating factors? How has this functionally impaired him?

On physical examination, remember to examine the hand, as well as possible causes more proximally.

2. Differential diagnosis should include carpal tunnel syndrome (CTS most likely, despite the history of entire hand pain – many patients do not present with a "classic" history of paresthesias in digits 1-3 and half of 4), ulnar neuropathy, cervical radiculopathy, ligament injury, tendonitis, thoracic outlet syndrome, and osteoarthritis. CTS is a clinical diagnosis and no further workup is required. However, to better characterize the extent of injury and possibly plan for surgical intervention given the weakness and atrophy noted, a NCS/EMG may be ordered. A bedside ultrasound may also be conducted to demonstrate significant swelling of the median nerve at the carpal tunnel compared to more proximal measurements.

3. EMG is useful here as it helps rule out an ongoing radiculopathy that may be responsible for his symptoms and localize symptoms (sampling both a proximal median-innervated muscle and a distal non-median innervated muscle). It also provides information on ongoing denervation, which appears to be present.

4. Patients may wish to exhaust conservative options before seeking a surgical opinion, which is not unreasonable as long as they understand the potential risk and benefit. However, make sure to have a close follow up plan in place, especially in light of his weakness.

References:

Huisstede, B. M., Randsdorp, M. S., Brink, J. V., Franke, T. P., Koes, B. W., & Hoogvliet, P. (2018). Effectiveness of Oral Pain Medication and Corticosteroid Injections for Carpal Tunnel Syndrome: A Systematic Review. Archives of Physical Medicine and Rehabilitation. doi:10.1016/j.apmr.2018.03.003

Burton, C., Chesterton, L. S., & Davenport, G. (2014). Diagnosing and managing carpal tunnel syndrome in primary care. British Journal of General Practice, 64(622), 262-263. doi:10.3399/bjgp14x679903

Pimentel, B. F., Faloppa, F., Tamaoki, M. J., & Belloti, J. C. (2018). Effectiveness of ultrasonography and nerve conduction studies in the diagnosing of carpal tunnel syndrome: Clinical trial on accuracy. BMC Musculoskeletal Disorders, 19(1). doi:10.1186/s12891-018-2036-4

Case: Parkinson's Disease

A 73-years-old male and his wife presents to your outpatient rehabilitation clinic as a referral from Neurology for Parkinson disease.

1. What information about the patient's history would you like to know in helping plan a rehabilitative program for him?

2. He was diagnosed with Parkinson's 2 years ago and is currently on carbidopa-levodopa as managed by his Neurologist. He reports a steady decline in his ability to walk, due to poor balance and coordination. He does not use any ambulatory devices. He has not had any recent falls, only several near-falls. Memory hasn't been an issue, although his wife notes his voice seems different than before. He has a resting tremor that interferes with his ability to use his hands, especially during eating, causing him significant frustration. He lives in a single-story home with his wife, who is in good health and assists him throughout the day. He doesn't currently exercise, aside from occasional walks, and is interested in learning any exercises that would help. His only other medical history consists of hypertension, and he has no prior surgeries or drug allergies. He denies any symptoms of depression or difficulty swallowing.

What information would you like to obtain on a focused physical examination?

3. He speaks quietly, slowly at times, but is alert and oriented, following all commands. His neurological examination is noted for normal strength aside from 4/5 hip flexors and hip extensors, normal sensation, diminished

facial expressions, hypophonia, and a resting tremor worse on his right, dominant side in the upper limbs. Arising from a seated to standing position is slow, and turning during ambulation is difficult. His gait is shuffling and delayed, appearing unsteady at times.

Describe your comprehensive rehabilitation plan for this patient.

4. You recommend a multi-disciplinary approach to rehabilitation, with goals of maintaining and/or improving function and alleviating caregiver burden through Physical Therapy to focus on lower limb strengthening, balance, gait training, and large movements, with a home exercise program. You also refer for a course of Occupational Therapy for adaptive equipment evaluation, especially for eating utensils to diminish impact of tremors (swivel, weighted, active cancellation of tremor eating devices), and consideration for home grab bars. Consider a referral to Speech Therapy to evaluate and treat hypophonia. Finally, you provide a walker to assist with balance and education on the role of therapy to manage symptoms of Parkinson disease.

The patient's wife mentions hearing about using stem cells to cure Parkinson disease and wonders about your opinion of this potential treatment – how do you respond?

5. At this time, there is no proven cure for Parkinson disease. Stem cell treatments are not an approved treatment for it, and they should be cautioned regarding providers that may prey on desperate patients and families with unproven treatments at a high financial cost. However, be sure to respond empathetically, not judgmentally, given their situation, and, if interested, provide information on

ongoing clinical trials for this condition, such as through ClinicalTrials.gov.

The patient and his wife are interested in learning more about Parkinson's and meeting others dealing with this disease process. How can you assist them with this?

6. Offer referrals to support groups and foundations, both nationally (such as American Parkinson Disease Association, Partners in Parkinson's, Parkinson's Foundation, and Michael J. Fox Foundation), and local community organizations that you may be aware of. Such organizations, especially on local levels, may help individuals understand their disease process and become less socially isolated through interactions with fellow patients and caregivers. They can also share experience and information through these interactions.

Notes:

1. Ascertain the history of Parkinson disease diagnosis, current and past treatment, and current functional ability. Be sure to explore the myriad of ways this disease may impact quality of life. Find out the current home situation, prior medical/surgical history, and if any acute injuries have occurred related to his current reason for referral.

2. A neurological examination should be conducted, with focus on strength, balance, gait, and ability to follow commands. Signs of Parkinson's should be documented, including tremor, masked facies, rigidity, and voice.

3. A comprehensive rehabilitation plan with referrals to multiple providers as well as extensive patient and

caregiver education is warranted. He has deficits in several areas (clearly gait is impaired placing him at a high-risk for falls and secondary complications), and while therapy alone will not stop the progression of Parkinson disease, it may help improve quality of life and function. Offer advice on home modifications that may diminish the risk of falls (such as ensuring pathways clear of obstacles like thick rugs, and also having nightlights available).

4. Questions regarding regenerative treatments are increasingly encountered by physiatrists. Remember to follow the medical principles of both beneficence and patient autonomy when responding, respecting their right to seek treatment, but also providing your expert advice regarding the limitations of such unproven therapy.

References:

Mcdonnell, M. N., Rischbieth, B., Schammer, T. T., Seaforth, C., Shaw, A. J., & Phillips, A. C. (2017). Lee Silverman Voice Treatment (LSVT)-BIG to improve motor function in people with Parkinson's disease: A systematic review and meta-analysis. *Clinical Rehabilitation*,026921551773438. doi:10.1177/0269215517734385

Monticone, M., Ambrosini, E., Laurini, A., Rocca, B., & Foti, C. (2015). In-patient multidisciplinary rehabilitation for Parkinsons disease: A randomized controlled trial. *Movement Disorders, 30*(8), 1050-1058. doi:10.1002/mds.26256

Case: Mixed Weakness

A 53-years-old male presents to your outpatient rehabilitation clinic reporting left hand and bilateral leg weakness.

1. What information about the patient's history would you like to find out to better ascertain the cause of presenting weakness?

2. His weakness started over the last year without any inciting event. He is left-hand dominant, notes progressive difficulty holding objects and opening jars with that hand, and denies paresthesias or pain. He cannot recall any alleviating or particularly aggravating factors. He thinks his legs are weaker as he can't get out of a chair as easily as before. He denies any recent injury to lower limbs, back pain, lower limb paresthesias, or changes to bowel or bladder function. He has no other medical history, prior surgical history, significant substance abuse, or toxin exposure. He notes some occasional hoarseness and coughing with eating. He denies any rashes, fevers, or associated trauma. He lives in a 2-story home with his wife. Describe your approach to a focused physical exam for this patient.

3. He is alert, oriented, and ambulates slowly. Skin inspection, palpation of spine, and range of motion examinations are unremarkable. He has difficulty arising from the examination chair. Strength in his upper limbs is within normal limits, except his distal finger flexors on left are 4-/5. His lower limb strength is also within normal limits, except for bilateral hip flexors, hip extensors, and quadriceps at 4/5. Sensation and reflexes are intact. Pulmonary auscultation is unremarkable. What is your

differential diagnosis? What additional workup would you recommend?

4. Differential diagnosis for a patient with painless, asymmetrical weakness includes neuromuscular junction disorder (myasthenic syndromes), myositis (polymyositis, inclusion body myositis, dermatomyositis), stroke, myelopathy, and motor neuron disease (ALS, Primary lateral sclerosis). Other diagnoses that may be considered such as GBS, polyradiculopathy, peripheral neuropathy, toxin exposure, and malignancy all less likely. Given the weakness, NCS/EMG should be utilized. The electrodiagnostic study returns with the nerve conduction study within normal limits, and the needle examination noting increased insertional activity, small amplitude motor units, and increased recruitment in multiple upper and lower limb muscles. How does this change your differential? What are your next steps in workup?

5. With these findings, concern for a myopathic cause of weakness should be investigated. CK is elevated, and muscle biopsy of a clinically weak muscle returns reporting rimmed vacuoles and mononuclear inflammatory cells entering non-necrotic muscle fibers. You diagnose inclusion body myositis. What is your comprehensive rehabilitation plan for the patient?

6. Start with providing education regarding the diagnosis to the patient. Referral to Neurology for evaluation for medication management (no current gold standard of pharmacologic treatment, use of steroid is typically not helpful, immunomodulating agents are controversial, but sometimes utilized). Physical therapy should be utilized, ideally with a therapist familiar with neuromuscular disorders, and for equipment needs, range of motion, and

improving mobility. Occupational therapy may be prescribed to address hand weakness and provide assistive devices for activities of daily living. Referral to Speech Therapy should be given for evaluation of possible swallow dysfunction (common in IBM) and treatment should also be done. As the disease progresses, consultation with Orthotics service for bracing should be considered. He expresses fear of this new diagnosis and asks, "Doc, is there any cure for this?"

7. Express sincere empathy regarding his current diagnosis and willingness to work with him to ensure his rehabilitative needs, including for equipment, are met. IBM currently does not have a cure and is a progressive disease. While patients with IBM may have a normal lifespan, patients with it typically develop significant disability with limited mobility and are at risk for aspiration pneumonia. However, therapy can improve quality of life and relief caregiver burden to an extent. Offer information on local and national support networks and resources for IBM. Finally, make sure he is aware you want to follow up regularly in clinic with him to address further concerns as they arise.

References:

Mazia, C. (2012). A 12-year follow-up in sporadic inclusion body myositis: An end stage with major disabilities. *Yearbook of Neurology and Neurosurgery, 2012*, 109-111. doi:10.1016/j.yneu.2011.12.002

Price, M. A., Barghout, V., Benveniste, O., Christopher-Stine, L., Corbett, A., Visser, M. D., . . . Tseng, B. S. (2016). Mortality and Causes of Death in Patients with Sporadic Inclusion Body Myositis: Survey Study Based on the Clinical Experience of Specialists in Australia, Europe and the USA. *Journal of Neuromuscular Diseases,3*(1), 67-75. doi:10.3233/jnd-150138

Amato, A. A., & Barohn, R. J. (2009). Inclusion body myositis: Old and new concepts. *Journal of Neurology, Neurosurgery & Psychiatry,80*(11), 1186-1193. doi:10.1136/jnnp.2009.173823

Case: Burn Injury

1. You are asked by a surgical team to evaluate a 33-years-old fast food restaurant employee who has been admitted to a local trauma center following a burn injury. What information would you like to know on history and physical examination? What are poor prognostic indicators for survival after a burn injury?

2. He experienced multiple burns over his arm and chest after a hot cooking oil scalding accident. He has no prior medical history or surgical history. He currently reports pain with movement and is receiving IV narcotics. On examination, he has second degree burns on his right upper limb, chest, and anterior left upper limb. His vitals are stable, heart and lung exam are unremarkable, and he is neurologically intact. He prefers not to move his upper limbs, but appears to have full range of motion. Your exam is limited by his reported pain. His primary team calculated his %Total Body Surface Area burned as approximately 25%. He weighs 70kg. A rotating medical student asks how much fluid he should receive upon admission. What is your response? Additionally, what rehabilitative needs are important to address?

3. The Parkland Formula is used to calculate fluid given to replace acute losses from a burn injury.

Rehabilitative needs following a burn injury are numerous and include:

Pain Management - pharmacologic and nonpharmacologic, to allow tolerance of therapy, dressing changes, and alleviate suffering. May include Patient Controlled Analgesia (PCA).

Contracture prevention - typically involves avoiding positions of comfort, with positioning of limbs in extension and abduction, and avoiding flexion and adduction. Splinting may be utilized.

Wound care - comprehensive wound management, specialized dressings along with potential debridement or skin grafting by surgical services/wound services.

Nutrition - optimizing nutrition to ensure maximal wound healing is vital. Increased caloric intake with additional vitamins (C, A) zinc, copper, and manganese.

Scar prevention - scars may contract and lead to both psychological and functional limitations. Minimizing this through use of compression garments (worn 23 hours/day, typically), steroids injected locally into scars, early mobilization, and silicone masks. Important in both acute and chronic phase as scar maturation may take up to 1.5 years.

Skilled therapy - deficits in mobility and ability to perform ADLs are likely. Once medically stable, order Physical Therapy and Occupational Therapy. Education for the patient, family, and care team regarding routine range of motion exercises is important.

Psychological assessment and support - burn injuries may result in significant loss of identity due to disfigurement. Connecting the patient with counseling, evaluating for depression, and considering peer support resources if recommended.

4. The patient completes his inpatient hospital stay and is discharged home. Two months later, the patient presents to your outpatient rehabilitation clinic on follow up. He reports continued stiffness at burn sites and scarring. He is

requesting replacement compression garments. The patient and his family are curious of any other complications associated with burn injury that they should be mindful of, and what they can do help prevent such issues? What validated tools are available to assess and track his scars?

Heterotopic ossification (H/O) is not uncommon following a burn injury, especially those with > 40% TBSA. The elbow is the most common location for formation of H/O in burn injuries. Regular ROM exercises and prompt evaluation should pain occur would be helpful.

Peripheral neuropathies, especially after electrical injuries, may occur. Education on the symptoms of neuropathies and positioning to avoid exacerbating any subclinical injuries would be recommended.

Psychological adjustment and sleep are continued issues to be screened for and addressed. Local and national support groups (such as the The Phoenix Society) for burn survivors may be considered.

Pruritus is very common following a burn injury, and using oral antihistamines would be recommended. Axonal sprouting in the dermis is a potential etiology.

Continued exercise with active ROM activities and regular stretching of skin contractures is vital.

Objective assessment tools for burn scars include the Vancouver Scar Scale (VSS, measurements of Vascularity, Pigmentation, Pliability, and Height) and the Patient and Observer Scar Assessment Scale (POSAS scale, with both patient perspective and scar examination measurements). A VSS height score of >1 or POSAS thickness score ≥ 3 may be considered hypertrophic and require additional interventions based on the scar surface area. Silicone, pressure dressing, intralesional corticosteroids, laser treatment, and even reconstructive surgery may be indicated.

5. Your department chief asks you to start a quality improvement project for the rehabilitative management of burn injuries during outpatient follow up. How would you proceed?

Review the latest evidence for rehabilitative interventions in burn injury and identify areas where improvements could be made, be it interventions or outcomes. Interview and partner with stakeholders, including clinical staff, referring physicians, therapists, and patients. Utilize the Plan, Do, Study, Act (PDSA) cycle of Quality Improvement. Ensure appropriate measurements of the initiated changes, and analyze the subsequent data after implementation to study effectiveness.

Notes:

>Second degree burns are characterized by damage to the epidermis and dermis.

>Third degree affect both as well as deeper tissue.

>Poor prognostic indicators for survival in burn care include age > 60, > 40% total body surface area burned, and the presence of inhalation injury.

>The Parkland formula is used to calculate how much fluid (Lactated ringer's) a patient may require with burn injuries:

[4mL x % Total Body Surface Area burned x Patient's Weight (kg)]

Of this, ½ is given in the first 8 hours, with the remaining ½ given in the next 16 hours.

Review the common components of a Quality Improvement project and be prepared to discuss them.

References:

Salisbury, R. (2012). Burn Scar Assessment: A Systematic Review of Different Scar Scales. *Yearbook of Plastic and Aesthetic Surgery, 2012*, 64. doi:10.1016/j.yprs.2011.02.041

Bloemen, M. C., Veer, W. M., Ulrich, M. M., Zuijlen, P. P., Niessen, F. B., & Middelkoop, E. (2009). Prevention and curative management of hypertrophic scar formation. *Burns, 35*(4), 463-475. doi:10.1016/j.burns.2008.07.016

Cuccurullo, S., & Lee, J. (2015). Physical Medicine and Rehabilitation Board Review. New York: Demos Medical.

Donovan, M. L., Muller, M. J., Simpson, C., Rudd, M., & Paratz, J. (2016). Interim pressure garment therapy (4–6 mmHg) and its effect on donor site healing in burn patients: Study protocol for a randomised controlled trial. *Trials,17*(1). doi:10.1186/s13063-016-1329-x

Gabriel, V., Holavanahalli, R., & Braddom, R. (2011). *Physical Medicine & Rehabilitation*. Philadelphia: Elsevier Saunders.

Case: Leg Weakness

1. A 48-years-old female presents to your clinic with reports of leg weakness. What information would you like to know on history and physical examination?

2. She reports weakness in her legs, progressively worsening over the last 6 months, without inciting event. She notes the weakness predominately with difficulty getting out of her office chair or when climbing stairs. Occasionally she feels her arms are weak as well, but her leg weakness is her primary concern. She has had a few near falls due to the weakness, but always has managed to catch herself and denies any trauma. Sometimes she feels her gait is "off." She denies any fevers, chills, numbness, tingling, pain, difficulty swallowing, although she does note a bothersome dry mouth and double vision recently. She has no significant past medical or surgical history, denies any current medications, and smokes 1 pack a day for the last 25 years. She feels the weakness is functionally limiting her ability to work and exercise.

On physical examination, she is alert, oriented, and without any muscle atrophy. She has 4/5 strength in her hip flexors and 5/5 strength distally. She has 5-/5 strength on shoulder abduction testing, and 5/5 distally, with normal sensation. Reflexes are diminished in upper and lower limbs, although Hoffman's and Babinski's are within normal limits. Skin exam is unremarkable and no synovitis is noted. Provocative maneuvers and ROM testing of the spine is within normal limits. Cranial nerve exam is significant for bilateral ptosis. What is your differential diagnosis and what is your next step in diagnostic workup?

3. Differential may include neuromuscular disorder (myopathy, motor neuron disease, IBM, myasthenic

syndrome), multiple sclerosis, spinal myelopathy. You order an NCS/EMG, and it returns showing diminished CMAP amplitudes, repetitive nerve stimulation with marked increase in CMAP amplitude, increase in amplitude after 10 seconds of maximal isometric muscle activation, and normal EMG of multiple muscle groups in the upper and lower limbs. What is your diagnosis? What is your treatment plan?

4. The diagnosis is likely Lamberton-Eaton Myasthenic Syndrome (LEMS). Given the significant association with underlying malignancy (especially with her smoking history), screening for such is needed urgently. CT chest, abdomen, pelvis is ordered, and returns noting a right-sided lung mass. Referrals to Neurology for possible pharmaceutical management of LEMS (pyridostigmine, possibly IVIG), and Oncology are needed. Extensive patient education regarding LEMS and its associated with malignancy is important, in addition to secondary prevention with smoking cessation. A course of Physical Therapy for limb strengthening, balance, fall recovery/fall prevention, and home exercise program development is prudent. Additionally, Occupational Therapy may be helpful for assistive devices to help diminish the burden imposed by her weakness.

The patient asks for your opinion on her prognosis. How do you respond?

5. Answer empathetically, noting the significance of this diagnosis and its impact on her. For patients with paraneoplastic LEMS, survival is typically shortened due to the underlying malignancy. Until tumor grade is noted by Oncology, exact prognosis is unknown. For those without

paraneoplastic LEMS, some evidence suggests lifespan is potentially near-normal, although significant disability may still occur. From a Rehabilitative standpoint, assurance that you will continue follow up to maximize her quality of life and functional ability is critical. You may consider referral to a Cancer Rehabilitation specialist as well.

Notes: Autonomic dysfunction, most commonly dry mouth, is often noted with LEMS. Ocular complaints also occur, but proximal muscle weakness is typically the key complaint for patients.

References:

Juel, V. C., & Sanders, D. B. (2012). The Lambert-Eaton Myasthenic Syndrome. *Myasthenia Gravis and Myasthenic Disorders,*156-172. doi:10.1093/med/9780199738670.003.0007

Oh, S. J. (2017). Distinguishing Features of the Repetitive Nerve Stimulation Test Between Lambert–Eaton Myasthenic Syndrome and Myasthenia Gravis, 50-Year Reappraisal. *Journal of Clinical Neuromuscular Disease,19*(2), 66-75. doi:10.1097/cnd.0000000000000190

Wirtz, P. W., Wintzen, A. R., & Verschuuren, J. J. (2005). Lambert–Eaton myasthenic syndrome has a more progressive course in patients with lung cancer. *Muscle & Nerve,32*(2), 226-229. doi:10.1002/mus.20332

Case: Dizziness

1. A 72-years-old woman is referred to you for dizziness "therapy" by her primary physician. What information would you like from her?

2. The dizziness started 2 months ago. She describes it as a sensation of the room spinning with associated mild nausea. She denies any trauma or injury related to the onset or afterwards during her dizzy spells. However, she has had a few near-falls due to the dizziness. She typically walks without any assistive device, although finds holding onto her friend's cane during these episodes is helpful, allowing her to still walk. Moving her head during episodes exacerbate symptoms, and sometimes brings on the sensation. Sometimes she notes ringing sensation in her ears during dizzy episodes, and these last a few seconds to around a minute. She notes mild functional limitation from these episodes, mostly from fear of falling. Review of system is negative for headaches, anxiety, recent illness, sensation of passing out, changes in vision, neck pain, chest pain, or shortness of breath.

She denies any prior medical history (including hearing loss), surgical history, drug allergies, or substance use. She exercises through daily walking. Her family history is unremarkable, but her best friend had a stroke at age 78, and she is concerned she may be having strokes that are causing this dizziness.

What information would you like on physical examination? What exam findings are important to elicit in differentiating central versus peripheral etiology of her symptoms?

3. Vital signs are within normal limits, including orthostatics. She ambulates on her own steadily, arises easily from a seated position, and her cardiac examination is unremarkable. A focused neurological examination, including cranial nerves, strength, sensation, reflexes, and cerebellar signs, is normal. Range of motion at the neck is also normal. With the patient's permission, you move her from sitting position to supine position, with her head at 45 degrees relative to the testing side and 20 degrees below the table once supine, watching for nystagmus, repeated in the opposite direction. You note horizontal and rotatory nystagmus that is fatigable and resolves in less than 1 minute, and she also reports reproduction of vertigo symptoms. What is the most likely diagnosis, and what next steps would you recommend?

4. You diagnose benign positional vertigo (BPV) as the most likely cause, a peripheral source of vertigo. Recommendations for management include educating the patient about the diagnosis and prognosis (typically resolves, although recurrence not uncommon), ordering an assistive device such as a single-point cane for safety with ambulation while treating episodes, referral to Physical Therapy for vestibular rehabilitation (including education on Epley maneuver, balance, fall prevention and recovery), home safety modifications to prevent falls (pathways clear of obstacles, nightlights available, etc.), and follow up plan. She states, "Doctor, thanks for explaining this to me – are you sure this isn't a stroke? Shouldn't I get an MRI?"

5. Acknowledge her concern, especially in light of her friend's stroke, and offer empathetic reassurance. Explain in lay terms that her history and physical exam clearly point towards a cause that is not from her central nervous system (brain) and that this is a common condition with typically

good outcomes. However, also note you will be happy to follow up closely in clinic with her to monitor for the development of any concerning findings and workup these if needed and offer to answer any further questions she may have.

Notes:

Dizziness is a common presenting complaint and a careful history and physical examination can point to peripheral versus central causes. Key components include characteristics of complaints (syncope vs. vertigo vs. lightheaded, triggered vs. spontaneous, episode length, etc.), any features of neurological dysfunction, other associated symptoms, and inciting triggers. Several helpful algorithms are available to differentiate between common causes (see references).

On physical examination, the Dix-Hallpike Maneuver may be especially helpful. Vertigo reproduction and nystagmus with the maneuver in a horizontal and/or rotational direction are commonly seen in BPV, but prolonged and not fatiguing nystagmus often with little vertigo is suggestive of a central cause. This exam technique should be done with caution due to movements involved, and it is important to screen patients for contraindications prior to performing it. Additionally, noting spontaneous nystagmus during cranial nerve exam that is primarily vertical suggests a central origin.

Rehabilitation options for BPV include focused therapy with repositioning (Epley's) education, in addition to general safety/fall prevention interventions. Dizziness may be very frightening, especially for otherwise healthy, aging individuals, and follow up to monitor symptom resolution is important. When answering this question that centers on patient communication (5), be sure to note your concern for her symptoms and your willingness to continue with workup as needed pending improvements.

References:

Muncie HL, Sirmans SM, James E. Dizziness: Approach to Evaluation and Management. Am Fam Physician. 2017;95(3):154-162.

Rashad, U. M. (2008). Long-term follow up after Epley's manoeuvre in patients with benign paroxysmal positional vertigo. The Journal of Laryngology & Otology, 123(01), 69. doi:10.1017/s0022215108002430

Pérez-vázquez P, Franco-gutiérrez V. Treatment of benign paroxysmal positional vertigo. A clinical review. J Otol. 2017;12(4):165-173.

Kim JS, Zee DS. Clinical practice. Benign paroxysmal positional vertigo. N Engl J Med. 2014;370(12):1138-47.

Kansu, L., Avci, S., Yilmaz, I., & Ozluoglu, L. N. (2010). Long-term follow-up of patients with posterior canal benign paroxysmal positional vertigo. Acta Oto-Laryngologica, 130(9), 1009-1012. doi:10.3109/00016481003629333

Case: Back Pain

1. A 34-years-old male presents to your office complaining of back pain. What information would you like to know on history and physical examination?

2. Back pain is localized to the low back, non-radiating, without paresthesias or weakness, and aching with stiffness in nature. He denies inciting event and notes the pain has been intermittent for the last 5 years, progressively worsening at times. Ibuprofen offers some relief as does hot showers. He works as a mechanic and pain is worse after long day. Substance abuse history is unremarkable. He denies any family history, prior surgical, or medical history. Neurological red flags on ROS are negative. He currently does not exercise. Physical exam is noted for normal vital signs, mild obesity with full ROM at lumbar spine, tenderness to palpation in lumbar paraspinals that reproduces pain, unremarkable provocative tests for nerve impingement, normal neurologic examination including Babinsky, and unremarkable Schober and Patrick's tests.

What additional workup would you recommend? What is your differential diagnosis?

3. X-rays of the lumbar spine maybe helpful (current guidelines per American College of Radiology do not recommend x-rays for low back pain without concerning findings on examination although expert opinion may differ). Further imaging is unlikely to be warranted in light of his presentation and examination at this time. Differential should include lumbar strain, lumbar myofascial dysfunction, lumbar spondylosis, with radiculopathy, myelopathy, inflammatory spondyloarthritis, malignancy, and infection possible, but less likely.

Lumbar x-rays show minimal degenerative changes. You diagnose lumbar myofascial dysfunction. What is your comprehensive rehabilitation plan?

4. Patient education regarding his diagnosis and likely prognosis is recommended. Following this, physical therapy for strengthening, stretching, modalities, posture, and instruction on a home exercise program is vital. Education on workplace ergonomics and lifting techniques would be helpful, especially given his line of employment. Education on diet, exercise, and weight management, possibly with a referral to Preventive Medicine physician, should be done. Finally, establish a follow-up plan for the patient to review therapy progress. Analgesics maybe considered, as may home modalities (TENS, heating pad, etc.).

At the conclusion of the visit, the patient turns to you and states, "Doc, I'm fine with working on this with PT, but I really would like to start with some pain medications first. My friend gave me his leftover Norco and it really made me feel good. Can't we just start with that?" How do you respond?

5. Requests for narcotics for the management of back pain are common. However, in light of increasing concerns over opioid prescribing habits and current back pain management guidelines, narcotics are not indicated for first-line use. First, establish recognition of the patient's concern and support for his interest in managing his back pain. Then, while reviewing his current diagnosis, discuss the importance of addressing the pain using the best rehabilitative interventions and nonpharmacologic modalities recommended at this time. Consideration for medications maybe offered, including topical analgesics, NSAIDs, Acetaminophen, possibly neuropathic agents as

well. Offer to schedule close follow-up to evaluate progress and make adjustments as necessary. Focus on the role of PM&R in improving function rather than purely pain management. You may note the significant dangers associated with medication abuse (taking from friends is classified as such, but address this in a non-confrontational and empathetic style). Failing other interventions, if opioids are to be started, review the need for establishing a pain contract and routine urine drug screening, potentially with consultation of a Pain Management specialist. This is a challenging, but often-encountered patient question in physiatric practice, and should be addressed with an emphasis on partnering with the patient to use all available resources to improve pain and function, while utilizing current best evidence to help guide practice and improve outcomes.

References:

Murphy, D. R., Schneider, M. J., Bise, C. G., & Justice, B. (2017). Noninvasive Treatments for Acute, Subacute, and Chronic Low Back Pain. *Annals of Internal Medicine, 167*(11), 833. doi:10.7326/l17-0471

Patel, N. D., Broderick, D. F., Burns, J., Deshmukh, T. K., Fries, I. B., Harvey, H. B., … Corey, A. S. (2016). ACR Appropriateness Criteria Low Back Pain. Journal of the American College of Radiology, 13(9), 1069–1078. https://doi.org/10.1016/j.jacr.2016.06.008

Case: Cerebral Palsy

1. While covering the inpatient rehabilitation unit, you are consulted on a 30-years-old female with a history of cerebral palsy. She has an implanted baclofen pump and the primary team is concerned it may be not be correctly functioning. What information would you like to know on history and physical examination?

2. She has a history of spastic tetraplegic cerebral palsy, with an intrathecal baclofen pump placed 3 years ago after failing oral antispasmodics and injections, and is currently managed by your rehabilitation clinic. She was admitted for a planned biopsy and workup of a kidney mass. She underwent an MRI several hours ago. At baseline, she ambulates on her own or with a cane, but prior to the pump often used a wheelchair outside of her home. She currently feels well, denies acute concerns including any itching, worsened spasticity, irritability, fevers, or confusion. On physical examination, her vitals are stable. She is alert and oriented without any delirium. Cardiac, abdominal, and pulmonary exams are unremarkable aside from small mass in right lower abdominal quadrant consistent with the pump. Neurologically, she has spasticity rated as MAS 1+ in the lower limbs and in her right upper limb, with sufficient strength for ambulation. What are you next steps and recommendations for the primary team?

3. You interrogate the baclofen pump, noting a motor stall occurred at the time of the MRI, followed by motor recovery shortly thereafter. You compare prior baclofen pump settings, including output and volume, with clinic records, noting consistency with prior programmed settings. Given that she is not demonstrating signs of baclofen withdrawal and it appears her pump has

appropriately restarted following the MRI, you note the low likelihood for malfunction at this time. You provide education to the patient and her team regarding signs of baclofen withdrawal to monitor for and to alert you of should they occur. Finally, you schedule a plan for routine follow-up in your clinic following her discharge.

In discussions with the primary inpatient team, they mention significant discomfort and a lack of understanding regarding the indications for baclofen pumps and subsequent management. They have heard such pumps have a high rate of complications and wonder why these are placed at all. How do you respond?

4. Intrathecal baclofen pump management may be challenging and require multi-specialty support, including physiatry, neurosurgery, and sometimes with consultation from device representatives. Complication rates as high as 40% within 3 years of implantation have been reported. Offer to provide educational in-services to the primary team staff regarding the basics of baclofen pumps, common complications, and the workup of such. Include nursing staff and other members of the patient care team, including therapists, and consider bringing sample pump devices if available. Discuss and emphasize your willingness and availability to partner with the primary team to ensure the best possible outcome for such patients.

Notes: With patients that have cerebral palsy, establish Gross Motor Function Classification Scores (GMCSF, in this case consistent with a 2), history of intrathecal baclofen pump, and current symptoms. Pump stall with MRI is common, but logs should indicate recovery. Reviewing prior records and settings is vital. Pump interrogation is important, but if high clinical suspicion for malfunction is present, further investigation possibly with catheter studies and neurosurgical consultation may be needed.

References:

Winter, G., Beni-Adani, L., & Ben-Pazi, H. (2018). Intrathecal Baclofen Therapy—Practical Approach: Clinical Benefits and Complication Management. *Journal of Child Neurology*,088307381878507. doi:10.1177/0883073818785074

Ghosh, D., Mainali, G., Khera, J., & Luciano, M. (2013). Complications of Intrathecal Baclofen Pumps in Children: Experience from a Tertiary Care Center. Pediatric Neurosurgery, 49(3), 138–144. https://doi.org/10.1159/000358307

Taira, T., Ueta, T., Katayama, Y., Kimizuka, M., Nemoto, A., Mizusawa, H., Tanabe, H. (2012). Rate of Complications Among the Recipients of Intrathecal Baclofen Pump in Japan: A Multicenter Study. Neuromodulation: Technology at the Neural Interface, 16(3), 266–272. https://doi.org/10.1111/ner.12010

Case: Knee Pain

1. A 77-years-old male presents to your rehabilitation clinic reporting persistent right knee pain. What information would you like to obtain on a focused history?

2. He had a right total knee replacement (TKA) 15 years ago, for severe osteoarthritis following several remote knee injuries and arthroscopic surgeries. His TKA postoperative course was uncomplicated and he was pleased with the surgery. However, over the last year the anterior and medial/lateral regions of the right have become painful, primarily with ambulation. He denies acute trauma. His left knee is starting to hurt as well, insidiously, over the last several months. Occasionally there is mild swelling at the right knee, without any fevers, chills, or erythema. Tylenol and ice offer temporary relief, but he is concerned as the knee has become more painful and occasionally unstable. Past surgical, medical, and family history is non-contributory. What information would you like on physical examination?

3. He is afebrile. He presents with an antalgic gait favoring his right knee. TKA surgical incision is well healed. Trace edema is noted at the right knee, and tenderness at medial and lateral joint lines is noted. No warmth or redness is appreciated, but increased laxity to varus stress testing is noted. Full ROM at the knee is present. Hip and ankle examination are unremarkable, as is the contralateral knee. What is your differential diagnosis and next steps in workup?

4. Differential includes prosthetic failure with aseptic loosening, prosthetic fracture, periprosthetic osteolysis, metallosis, knee hardware infection, and you also may

consider much less likely referred pain from lumbar radiculopathy, hip pathology or ankle pathology. Further workup includes scan, CBC, ESR, CRP, and x-rays (possibly CT scan) of the right knee.

5. Lab workup returns unremarkable. X-ray and CT scan demonstrate changes concerning for TKA prosthesis loosening. What is your next step?

6. You refer the patient to Orthopedic surgery for evaluation and possible surgical intervention. Additionally, you offer extensive patient education regarding the findings of your workup, as well as oral analgesics to assist with pain relief, and a cane to help unload the problematic knee. Several weeks later, he follows up with you, and reports an upcoming knee surgery after completing his Orthopedic evaluation. He expressed frustration regarding the outcome of his prior total knee replacement and states he wants to sue his past surgeon. He asks if you think he has a case. How do you respond?

7. Express recognition and understanding of how frustrating this situation is for him. Note you cannot comment on the actions of other physicians, that knee replacements typically have a lifespan, and recommend focusing on moving forward with his care. Advise him that you are not an attorney and cannot offer legal guidance. Note the importance of continued follow up with yourself and his surgical team, including after the surgery is complete. Discuss the need for further rehabilitation and planning for the road ahead following a possible TKA revision.

References:

Kim, K. T., Lee, S., Ko, D. O., Seo, B. S., Jung, W. S., & Chang, B. K. (2014). Causes of Failure after Total Knee Arthroplasty in Osteoarthritis Patients 55 Years of Age or Younger. Knee Surgery & Related Research, 26(1), 13–19. https://doi.org/10.5792/ksrr.2014.26.1.13

Artz, N., Elvers, K. T., Lowe, C. M., Sackley, C., Jepson, P., & Beswick, A. D. (2015). Effectiveness of physiotherapy exercise following total knee replacement: systematic review and meta-analysis. BMC Musculoskeletal Disorders, 16(1). https://doi.org/10.1186/s12891-015-0469-6

Luque, R., Rizo, B., Urda, A., Garcia-Crespo, R., Moro, E., Marco, F., & López-Duran, L. (2014). Predictive factors for failure after total knee replacement revision. International Orthopaedics, 38(2), 429–435. https://doi.org/10.1007/s00264-013-2268-8

Jasper, L. L., Jones, C. A., Mollins, J., Pohar, S. L., & Beaupre, L. A. (2016). Risk factors for revision of total knee arthroplasty: a scoping review. BMC Musculoskeletal Disorders, 17(1). https://doi.org/10.1186/s12891-016-1025-8

Case: Shoulder Pain

A 34-year-old male presents to your outpatient clinic with a complaint of shoulder pain.

1. What history would you like to know?

The patient is a right-handed male construction worker that plays recreational baseball on the weekends. He reports his pain started gradually over 5 months and does not recall specific injuries before the onset of pain. His pain is gradually becoming more frequent, and he has trouble with overhead movements due to sharp pain. This pain has limited him from participating in his recreational baseball in the last month. Stopping this activity has not helped his pain. He has not had any treatment so far. He denies neck pain. There are no paresthesias down the arms.

2. What physical examination would you do?

There are no signs of atrophy to the upper extremities, chest and back regions. There is a prominent medial border of his right scapula with signs of scapular dyskinesia. There is tenderness to palpation to the right coracoid process, nontender to the region of the biceps tendon. He has full active shoulder range of motion with pain starting in abduction at 90 to 120 degrees. Upper extremity strength, reflexes and sensation are intact. Special testing of the shoulder is positive for Neer's, empty can and full can tests. Empty can and full can test become less painful with the scapular support maneuver. O'brien's and drop arm tests are negative. Cervical examination including range of motion is unremarkable .

3. Based on the history and physical exam findings, what is your differential diagnosis?

SICK scapula syndrome, Shoulder impingement syndrome, Rotator cuff syndrome, Supraspinatus tear, Calcific tendonitis, Shoulder labral tear, Brachial plexus injury, Long thoracic nerve injury, or a Pancoast tumor.

4. What diagnostics would you order for this patient?

Shoulder X-rays to evaluate alignment, fracture, predisposition of impingement, calcific tendonitis. May also consider cervical X-ray to rule out possible cervical pathology, and an in-clinic ultrasound to evaluate possible rotator cuff injury and dynamic impingement. Finally, may consider MRI for shoulder if refractory to treatment.

5. Assuming the diagnosis is SICK scapula syndrome, what is your plan for management?

SICK scapula syndrome (**S**capular malposition, **I**nferior medial border prominence, **C**oracoid pain, scapular dys**K**inesia) is a common condition in overhead athletes, and the main treatment for this is physical therapy. This includes scapular stabilization, motor re-education, and instruction for home exercise program for patient self-management. Medications including topicals and NSAIDs. Consideration for relative rest from his sporting activity with gradual return to play as he becomes more pain free. Consideration of work restrictions/modifications with overhead lifting given his work in construction. Consider injections for pain control if unable to tolerate therapy.

6. The patient reports that he has been recommended a TENS unit from his physical therapist, which was denied by insurance. How would you approach this situation?

Offer to call his insurance company about the denial of the device. Consider drafting an appeal letter to send to the insurance company. Call the treating physical therapist to discuss alternative modalities that may be covered that can provide the same relief/goals. Advise the patient on potential over-the-counter alternative TENS units that can be obtained for marginal cost.

7. Roleplaying the situation: The patient comes into your clinic requesting stem cell injections as he feels that it would help him return to also playing as a star recreational baseball pitcher. How would you advise him to proceed?

Be empathetic that the patient has a strong desire to return to play. Inquire about what he has heard about "stem cells", clarify any misconceptions regarding regenerative medicine techniques. Advise that most of these techniques are still investigational and unlikely to return him to play quicker. Practice active listening and discuss his concerns before offering guidance and alternatives that are more in line with the standard of care.

References:

Struyf, F., Nijs, J., Mottram, S., Roussel, N. A., Cools, A. M., & Meeusen, R. (2014). Clinical assessment of the scapula: a review of the literature. British journal of sports medicine, 48(11), 883-890.

Nowotny, J., Kasten, P., Kopkow, C., Biewener, A., & Mauch, F. (2018). Evaluation of a new exercise program in the treatment of scapular dyskinesis. International journal of sports medicine, 39(10), 782-790.

Pas, H. I., Moen, M. H., Haisma, H. J., & Winters, M. (2017). No evidence for the use of stem cell therapy for tendon disorders: a systematic review. British journal of sports medicine, 51(13), 996-1002.

Mora, M. V., Ibán, M. A. R., Heredia, J. D., Laakso, R. B., Cuéllar, R., & Arranz, M. G. (2015). Stem cell therapy in the management of shoulder rotator cuff disorders. World Journal of Stem Cells, 7(4), 691.

Case: Hip Crepitation

A 29-year-old female presents to your outpatient clinic with a complaint of hip pain.

1. What history would you like to know?

The patient is a professional dancer that noticed left anterior hip pain with the feeling of clicking and snapping increasing in frequency over the past 3 months. She does not recall any previous specific injury to the region. She reports more pain with hip flexion and difficulty with deep squatting due to this intermittent pain. She denies radiation of the hip pain. She denies ankle, knee and low back pain. She denies lower extremity paresthesias. She reports use of NSAIDs without change to her symptoms.

2. What physical examination would you do?

No signs of atrophy to the lower extremities, abdominal and back region. There is tenderness to palpation to the iliotibial band and the region of the AIIS. The lumbar region is nontender to palpation. She has full active hip and knee range of motion. Lower extremity strength, reflexes and sensation are intact. Special testing of the hip region is positive for left Stinchfield test and left Ober's test are positive. Left FABER with reproduction of her anterior snapping sensation. Snapping can be felt with palpation along the left anterior hip during the Thomas test. The FAIR, log roll, and hip scour tests are negative. There is no lumbar pain with range of motion, lumbar special testing is unremarkable. Sacroiliac joint special testing is unremarkable.

3. Based on the history and physical exam findings, what is your differential diagnosis?

Snapping hip syndrome, Iliotibial band syndrome, Quadriceps strain, Iliopsoas strain, hip osteoarthritis, femoral acetabular impingement syndrome, lumbar radiculopathy, greater trochanteric pain syndrome, Sacroiliac joint pain, and Hip septic joint

4. What diagnostics would you order for this patient?

Bilateral hip XR to examine possible hip pathology, lumbar XR to evaluate causes of referred pain. Clinical ultrasound of the left hip for examination of tendons, ligaments and dynamic stability. Consider MRI hip for refractory cases.

5. Assuming the diagnosis is snapping hip syndrome, what is your plan for management?

Physical therapy for targeted muscle stretching and motor control re-education of the hip and pelvis region. Modalities, topical and oral medications consideration for symptomatic snapping hip. Consider injections. If refractory to conservative consider surgical referral.

6. The patient reports she has difficulty attending physical therapy due to her demands at work. How would you help her?

Consider referral to physical therapy with more accommodating hours. Offer instruction in a home exercise program as an alternative. Discuss ways to help her with time off from work including an off-work letter and work restrictions.

7. Roleplaying the situation: The patient returns to your clinic reporting that physical therapy taught her nothing that she did not already know as a dancer. She is demanding surgical referral. How do you respond?

Be empathetic that the patient has a strong desire to return to her normal activities. Inquire about what happened at physical therapy, and clarify any misconceptions regarding goals of therapy. Practice active listening and discuss her concerns. Consider offering alternatives such as injections and possible referral for surgical consultation.

References:

Wunderbaldinger, P., Bremer, C., Matuszewski, L., Marten, K., Turetschek, K., & Rand, T. (2001). Efficient radiological assessment of the internal snapping hip syndrome. European radiology, 11(9), 1743-1747.

Musick, S. R., & Varacallo, M. (2017). Snapping hip syndrome.

Yen YM, Lewis CL, Kim YJ. Understanding and treating the snapping hip. Sports medicine and arthroscopy review. 2015 Dec;23(4):194.

Via, A. G., Fioruzzi, A., & Randelli, F. (2017). Diagnosis and management of snapping hip syndrome: A comprehensive review of literature. Rheumatology (Sunnyvale), 7(228), 2161-1149.

Case: Elbow Pain

A 41-year-old construction worker presents to your outpatient rehabilitation clinic as a referral from primary care with right elbow pain.

1. What information about the patient's history and physical examination would you like to know?

He is right hand dominant and has worked in construction for 20 years and he uses heavy power tools daily. He has had elbow pain for 4 weeks and has not had a specific injury or trauma. He had similar symptoms about 10 years ago that resolved without intervention. He describes symptoms of radiating pain on the "outside elbow" down the forearm that is worse with wrist extension under resistance, and when gripping tools. His pain ranges from mild-to-severe and is exacerbated with use. The once intermittent pain is now constant. His grip feels weak compared to the left, and he does not have forearm or hand sensory changes. He tried over-the-counter oral NSAIDs with no relief. On focused examination, he has marked tenderness over extensor carpi radialis brevis (ECRB) at or near the lateral epicondyle. Pain is reproduced with resisted wrist extension[a], middle finger extension[b], and elbow extension with pronation and passive wrist flexion. Elbow range of motion is normal. There is no gross deformity or effusion of the elbow joint. Sensory and motor examination are normal with exception to pain induced weakness of wrist and finger extensors.

2. What do you think is the most likely diagnosis?

Lateral epicondylitis (LE) "tennis elbow" is most likely with the history and physical examination findings. An advanced differential for elbow pain can be developed with consideration to location. Other causes of lateral pain may include ligamentous injury, osteochondral defect, plica, posterolateral rotatory instability, anconeus strain, and radial tunnel syndrome/posterior interosseous nerve syndrome. Posteriorly olecranon bursitis, olecranon fracture, and triceps tendonitis. Medially consider valgus extension overload, medial epicondylitis, ligamentous injury (ulnar collateral ligament), and ulnar nerve entrapment. Anteriorly biceps tendonitis and pronator syndrome. Lastly, arthritis (inflammatory or degenerative) should also be considered.

3. How will you manage this patient? Describe a comprehensive rehabilitation plan.

Non-operative management for LE represents first-line treatment, though current consensus on an optimal approach to treatment options is lacking. Generally, LE is self-limiting and resolves within 12- to 18-months without treatment. Some may benefit from additional non-operative care that often includes topical nonsteroidal anti-inflammatory medication, counterforce bracing, and physical therapy. Therapeutic goals are controlling elbow pain, preserving movement of the affected limb, improving grip strength, and preventing further deterioration.

NSAIDs may be helpful in the first 4 weeks of treatment with preference of topical NSAIDS to reduce cardiovascular and GI side effects. Biomechanically, immobilizing the forearm can significantly lessen tension on the affected ECRB, thereby facilitating self-repair. Counterforce brace is the most common and can significantly reduce pain caused by the extensor muscles. In addition, wrist cock-up braces used during ADLs can limit wrist extension and firing of the ECRB allowing the injured tendon to heal. Physical therapy may incorporate eccentric strengthening exercises, extracorporeal shockwave therapy, phonophoresis, and ergonomic education to improve pain and restore function.

Providers may also cautiously consider corticosteroid injection, Platelet-enriched plasma (PRP), and acupuncture for pain control.

Surgical intervention is available for recalcitrant cases.

4. How would you inform the patient who is asking for a corticosteroid injection about the efficacy of this option? What if your patient asks about PRP or acupuncture?

Steroid injections are controversial with poor long-term efficacy and potential adverse effects. Compared to patients doing physical therapy alone, those receiving steroid injections may have short term relief of pain. However, at 1-year follow up, there appears to be no difference in outcome in therapy only to the injection and therapy. Notably, repeated injections carry risk of iatrogenic tendon rupture, muscle atrophy, and cosmetic loss of skin pigmentation at the injection site.

Advise the patient that, although PRP has gained popularity in recent years, studies have reported conflicting results of benefit. Caution the patient against over promised results from this type of intervention, especially if it carries a high financial burden for him, but also support his autonomy in pursing this option.

Acupuncture is beneficial in many musculoskeletal disorders but is not a proven pain management option for LE.

5. The patient would like to return to work and would like to know if he should expect recurrence. How would you educate him?

The recurrence rate of LE is 8% at 2-years. To deter or prevent recurrence, the etiology of the condition must be considered. For this patient, it is likely use of heavy power tools repetitively. You may see if he has looked at equipment alternatives (lighter weight, different grips). Job modifications may be necessary and may be facilitated by a job site evaluation. Ask the patient about his specific job duties so you can provide individualized work accommodations as necessary for him during recovery. Investigation into avocational activities is also important because other contributing factors to this condition may be identified. In addition, educate him about adherence to a home exercise program as a key strategy in reducing rate of recurrence.

Notes: Common risk factors include age >40, overuse and repetitive activities, past medical history of LE, and poor mechanics during occupational or hobby activities.

LE is usually a clinical diagnosis. For refractory cases or to exclude other cause, x-rays, MRI, or CT can be ordered. EMG should be considered in refractory cases, especially if PIN muscles (including extensor indices) are weak on examination. Ultrasound is a user-dependent, emerging diagnostic tool used in clinical settings.

LE is not an inflammatory process. Though the exact pathophysiology is unknown, there is substantial evidence describing a degenerative process (microtearing and hypoperfusion) of the ECRB and common extensor tendons leading to histological changes.

References:

Sims S, Miller K, Elfar J, and Hammert W. Non-surgical treatment of lateral epicondylitis: a systematic review of randomized controlled trials. Hand. 2014 Dec;9(4):419-46. doi:10.1007/s11552-014-9642-x.

Lapner P et al. Non-operative treatment of lateral epicondylitis; A systematic review and meta-analysis. JSES International. 2021 Dec. doi: 10.1016/j.jseint.1021.11.010.

Ma K and Wang HQ. Management of lateral epicondylitis: a narrative literature review. Pain Res manag. May 2020;2020;6965381. doi: 10.1155/2020/6965381.

Kane S, Lynch J, and Taylor J. Evaluation of elbow pain in adults. Am Fam Physician. 2014 Apr 15;89(8):649-657.

Buchanin K and Varacallo M. Tennis elbow. StatPearls. https://www.ncbi.nlm.nih.gov/books/NBK431092

Case: Heel Pain

A 46-year-old female presents to your office with bilateral heel pain that has been worsening and she is having difficulty walking.

1. What additional information would you like to know about her history and physical examination?

She has had bilateral heel pain, right equal to left, for 2 weeks. She just started a power walk class with friends to lose weight – her BMI is 35. Her pain is worse in the morning with the first few steps getting out of bed and when walking barefoot. Complete weight bearing in the morning is very painful, so she uses a borrowed cane to offload full weight. Her pain generally improves over the course of the day but returns in the evening or after prolonged rest. She has not tried anything for her symptoms except submerging her feet in 10-minute ice baths once a day. On focused physical examination there is no bruising, effusion, or ecchymosis by inspection; she has pes planus bilaterally. Tenderness to palpation is appreciated over the calcaneus and mid arch, with very mild tenderness over the metatarsals bilaterally. She does not have tenderness medially or laterally over the ankle joint or ligamentous structures of the ankle (deltoid ligament, ATFL, CFL). Passive range of motion is painful when dorsiflexed to end-range and there is tightness of the gastrocnemius; passive extension of the toes provokes her pain. Motor and sensory examination is normal. Reflexes are normal.

2. What is your differential diagnosis and what additional work-up would you want?

The most likely diagnosis is plantar fasciitis (PF). Tenderness over the calcaneus is almost obligatory in this condition. It is also common to have mid-arch tenderness. Other possibilities would be a calcaneal stress fracture, heel spur, metatarsalgia, posterior tibialis tendinopathy, heel pad syndrome, Achilles' tendinopathy, and ankle arthritis (inflammatory and degenerative). Given no sensory involvement or weakness, nerve conditions such as S1 radiculopathy, neuroma, and tarsal tunnel syndrome are much less likely. Others such as fibular tendinopathy, sinus tarsi, and plantar warts would not explain this patient's symptoms.

In this case, a diagnosis of PF can be made based on clinical symptoms. Radiographs can be helpful in excluding other etiologies of heel pain but are typically unnecessary for diagnosis. MRI or advanced imaging is not warranted on this initial visit.

3. What is your comprehensive rehabilitation plan for this patient?

In many cases, PF is self-limiting with resolution within 12-months in 90% of the population. Relative rest and stretching before weight bearing can be recommended along with a referral to physical therapy to address the biomechanical contributors (gait assessment), stabilization (extrinsic and intrinsic foot muscles), stretching (gastrocnemius), arch taping, modalities (ultrasound or iontophoresis) and HEP. Pain can typically be controlled conservatively with icing or a short course of OTC medications (NSAIDs, acetaminophen). Refer her for OTC or custom soft heel or arch supports to reduce stress to the plantar fascia. Heel lifts can provide short-term relief but increase risk for heel cord shortening if used too long. Full evaluation of shoe wear to help minimize abnormal foot motion during physical activity would also be prudent. Discuss diet and exercise alternatives for weight loss such as water-based activities.

4. Patient returns to your office 6-months later and says her symptoms have lessened, but she still has morning pain. She would like to know what else can be done.

Reexamine the patient and verify diagnosis. Ask her about the effectiveness of the recommendations from the last visit and her consistency with HEP. Consider x-rays (spurs, arthritis) or advanced imaging given refractory symptoms. Night splinting for chronic PF may help. Steroid injections have been used with varied efficacy. Referrals to podiatry or ortho/sports medicine may also be considered if symptoms do not improve despite conservative care. Don't forget to ask her about her weight loss journey and offer a referral to a nutritionist or dietician if she is interested.

5. Patient is an administrative assistant and works long hours at her desk. Her pain is worse when she sits too long so she tries to walk around to stretch often. Her employer says she must stay at her desk for customer service unless she's on a break. How can you help this patient?

Through active listening, a spirit of advocacy and partnership, ask the patient if it would help for you to provide her employer a letter outlining necessary work accommodations. Inform the patient that she can call you if she has any trouble and her employer can call you with any questions. This would also be a good time to review stretching exercises that can be done while she is sitting at her desk.

Notes: In refractory cases, after x-rays, MRI is the imaging of choice and may show plantar fascia thickening and tears. The advantage of an MRI is evaluation of other foot and ankle structures. CT is not typically recommended unless suspicious for fracture.

References:

Tu P. Heel Pain: Diagnosis and Management. Am Fam Physician. 2018 Jan 15;97(2):86-93.

Berbrayer D. Plantar Fasciitis. PM&R knowledge now. May 2020 last updated. https://now.aapmr.org.

Morrissey D, Cotchett M, Sid J'Bari A, *et al.* Management of plantar heel pain: a best practice guide informed by a systematic review, expert clinical reasoning and patient values. British Journal of Sports Medicine. 2021;55:1106-1118.

Draghi F, Gitto S, Bortolotto C, Draghi A, and Belometti G. Imaging of plantar fascia disorders: findings on plain radiography, ultrasound and magnetic resonance imaging. 2016 Dec. PMID 27957702. doi: 10.1007/s13244-016-0533-2.

Case: Hip Pain

A 40-year-old male is in acute rehab after a motor vehicular polytrauma accident with reported new onset left hip pain on morning rounds.

1. What history would you like to know?

Review of injuries sustained include right tibial, fibula, and acetabular fracture now status post ORIF. He was GCS 14 at the scene of the MVA. He is on Norco PRN for pain control. He has been participating in physical and occupational therapy over his current rehab stay, until the last week where therapy has noted right hip pain and restricted range of motion is limiting gains with transfers and gait training.

2. What physical examination would you do?

No signs of atrophy to the lower extremities. Surgical wound sites are clean, intact, and dry. Noted swelling and warmth to the right hip region without redness. There is tenderness to palpation in the right hip region. The lumbar region is nontender to palpation. Left extremity range of motion is limited by pain. Right knee and ankle range of motion is within normal limits. Right hip is restricted hip flexion, extension and abduction, examination of range of motion is limited by pain. Lower extremity reflexes and sensation are intact. Distal strength in the right lower extremity is intact. Bilateral hip strength, left knee and ankle strength are limited by pain. Special testing of the hip region is pan positive. There is a general feeling of soreness in the lumbar region with range of motion, and lumbar special testing is unremarkable.

3. Based on the history and physical exam findings, what is your differential diagnosis?

Heterotopic ossification of the right hip, Deep Vein Thrombosis, Right hip fracture, Iliotibial band syndrome, Septic joint, Cellulitis, Iliopsoas strain, Adductor strain, Lumbar radiculopathy, and Lumbar stenosis.

4. What diagnostics would you order for this patient?

Bilateral hip XR to examine possible hip pathology. Lumbar XR to evaluate causes of referred pain. Bilateral Ultrasound Duplex in consideration for possible DVT. Triple Phase Bone Scan for early detection of heterotopic ossification. Infectious work up labs to exclude infectious etiologies.

5. Assuming the diagnosis is heterotopic ossification, what is your plan for management?

NSAIDs, pain control with medications, modalities, and injections. Physical therapy for range of motion. Consider repeat imaging as an outpatient 6 to 12 months later to determine maturity of the heterotopic ossification and possible surgical referral for removal if there is significant impairment in range of motion, and/or pain limiting function.

6. The patient has overstayed his estimated length of stay and he is currently moderate assist for transfers. He does not have anyone that can take care of him 24/7 as his wife has to work. How would you approach this situation?

Call the insurance company to advocate for an extension in length of stay. Explain that there is a new diagnosis of heterotopic ossification and given his function he would benefit for range of motion exercises and pain control. Assess alternative discharge plans including skilled nursing stay, home health options, and friends and other family members that may be able to help. Setup family training with identified care givers.

7. Roleplaying the situation: The patient's wife is at bedside and angry that the physician prior had missed the fracture in his right hip. How do you respond?

Be empathetic and practice active listening about the patient and his wife's concerns by paraphrasing what was said by the patient and his loved ones then offering correcting statements about misconceptions. Explain that heterotopic ossification is a bone formation around places that do not typically have bone. This can happen after a trauma such as the car accident that he was in. Also, explain that although the exact way this happens is not fully understood, but this occurs after the accident, not during. Explain the process of prevention and treatment options.

References:

Bossche LV, Vanderstraeten G. Heterotopic ossification: a review. J Rehabil Med. 2005 May;37(3):129-36.

Juarez, J. K., Wenke, J. C., & Rivera, J. C. (2018). Treatments and Preventative Measures for Trauma-Induced Heterotopic Ossification: A Review. Clinical and translational science, 11(4), 365–370. https://doi.org/10.1111/cts.12552

Case: Chest Pain

A 45-year-old male presents to your outpatient clinic with a complaint of chronic intermittent lower chest pain.

1. What history would you like to know?

The patient is a jujitsu instructor who reports right-sided lower chest pain. The pain is sharp and intermittent. He has had this for 4-5 years, and reports he first felt it after a pop in his chest when he was held in a Kimura jujitsu hold. Since this injury he has had the condition flare up monthly. It is made worse with right arm movements, twisting movements, deep breathing, and coughing when it is present. He does not have radiation of pain down his arms. He reports initially after the injury he went to the ER and was told there were no fractures. Subsequently he has had return visits to the ER for workup of potential myocardial infarction which have been negative. He manages the pain with NSAIDs and relative rest.

2. What physical examination would you do?

Palpation to right ribs 8-10 are painful. There is less rib excursion on the right side with inhalation and exhalation. Upper chest, low back, T and L spine are nontender. Normal lumbar range of motion. Normal right shoulder range of motion. Normal heart and breath sounds. Special testing of the right shoulder is unremarkable. Special testing of the lumbar region is unremarkable. The hooking maneuver test for the right ribs 8-10 reproduce pain.

3. Based on the history and physical exam findings, what is your differential diagnosis?

Slipping Rib Syndrome, Costochondritis, Tietze syndrome, Abdominal/Oblique Strain, Latissimus Strain, Rib Fracture, Angina, Cholelithiasis, Myocardial infraction, and Pneumonia.

4. What diagnostics would you order for this patient?

Rib Series XR in consideration for fracture. Chest XR for possible heart and lung pathology. Lumbar and Thoracic XR for possible spine pathology. MRI lumbar and thoracic spine if suspecting intraspinal canal pathology or radiculopathy. Abdominal ultrasound for liver and gall bladder pathology. EKG for possible cardiac causes.

5. Assuming the diagnosis is slipping rib syndrome, what is your plan for management?

Physical therapy for core stability, possible rib and thoracic spine mobilization, as tolerated. Rib binding/bracing. Modalities, topical and oral medications consideration for symptomatic rib pain. Diagnostic blocks for confirmation of rib pain may be helpful. In rare refractory cases consider orthopedic referral.

6. You receive a call from an agent from the US Olympic association inquiring about the status of your patient's injury. How do you respond?

Get the agency representative to identify themselves. Do not confirm or deny that the patient is under your care, as per HIPPA guidelines you are not allowed to disclose this information without permission. Advise that the agent must obtain release of records through the patient in question and medical records will only be furnished with appropriate signed written consent from the patient.

7. Roleplaying the situation: The patient returns to your clinic reporting that he recalls that he hurt his ribs at his workplace. He is requesting that you write a letter to his employer to support his claim. How would you respond?

Be empathetic. Practice active listening and discuss his concerns. Document his history of injury in the medical record and advise that his medical record is available for him to forward to his employer, legal team, and health providers with his consent. Advised that you are not a legal professional and are not involved typically with work claims and that he should seek advice from his employer or legal counsel.

References:

Heinz, G. J., & Zavala, D. C. (1977). Slipping rib syndrome: Diagnosis using the hooking maneuver. JAMA, 237(8), 794-795.

McMahon, L. E. (2018, June). Slipping rib syndrome: a review of evaluation, diagnosis and treatment. In Seminars in pediatric surgery (Vol. 27, No. 3, pp. 183-188). WB Saunders.

Van Tassel, D., McMahon, L. E., Riemann, M., Wong, K., & Barnes, C. E. (2019). Dynamic ultrasound in the evaluation of patients with suspected slipping rib syndrome. Skeletal radiology, 48(5), 741-751.

Case: Inpatient Multiple Sclerosis

A 30-year-old female is admitted to your inpatient rehabilitation unit following hospitalization for an exacerbation of multiple sclerosis.

1. What would you like to know about this patient's history and physical examination?

She was diagnosed with relapsing-remitting multiple sclerosis (MS) 5-years ago by her neurologist who saw lesions (white matter plaques) on her brain MRI. She has been on Copaxone for the last year. She lives with her husband in a 2-story home, and she has 2 young children. She works as a schoolteacher and enjoys her job. At baseline, she is modified independent with mobility and she is independent with ADLs. She has had many relapses since being diagnosed, and so far, she has had near complete return to baseline level of function each time. She uses a cane for balance and has had a few falls at home, mostly climbing the stairs. During this hospitalization, she was treated for a MS exacerbation and had complications of hospital acquired PNA that increased her length of stay. She feels much weaker compared to her baseline. She has been working with physical therapy and is min/mod assist with bed mobility, transfers, and gait using a front wheeled walker. On examination, she has proximal greater than distal lower and upper limb weakness. Sensory is abnormal in the right arm in a patchy distribution. Her reflexes are brisk throughout. Babinski's and Hoffman's are positive. Her tone is normal to slightly increased. She does not have nystagmus and cranial nerves are normal. Her vital signs are stable.

2. What would be your comprehensive rehabilitation plan for this patient?

This patient would benefit from a multidisciplinary care approach. You would order physical therapy (progressive resistive exercises, gait, neuromuscular retraining, proprioception, ROM, stair management) and occupational therapy (ADL's and adaptive equipment) for functional restoration. She will be evaluated for household durable medical equipment (shower chair, raised toilet seat, grab bars, shower bench) and most appropriate mobility device (cane, front wheeled walker, four wheeled walker or wheelchair).

Include vision rounds/optometry/ophthalmology, if available, given the high association of visual disturbances in this population (nystagmus, optic nerve lesions and inflammation). Psychology/Psychiatry may help her with adjustment and mental health (depression, anxiety). Speech therapy if cognitive or swallow issues are identified. Social work services may be involved to assist with in-home resources should it be necessary. Many patients find chaplain services comforting and one should consider asking the patient's interest in community or hospital-based MS support groups. Monitor for ongoing medical stability, bladder dysfunction, and ensure adequate pain control.

3. The patient develops worsening spasms, vision changes with eye pain, and has regression of function. What would be the appropriate next steps?

Complete a comprehensive neurological assessment and initiate medical work-up for cause. Often infections can mimic disease progression and should be ruled out urgently. You may order CBC with diff, CMP, ESR, CRP, lactate, procalcitonin, urinalysis and chest x-ray. Consider supplemental oxygen if oxygen saturations are less than 90%, or for comfort if patient is short of breath. Also, consult neurology as this is likely a recurrent exacerbation and she will need treatment (i.e., corticosteroids, IVIg or plasma exchange therapy) on the neurology service. Be sure you keep the patient and the family updated on findings.

4. Your patient transfers off service to be treated for a urinary tract infection and optic neuritis. One week later there is a consult for readmission to rehab. She really wants to come, but her insurance has denied it based on lack of medical necessity. What will you do?

First, review the functional and medical documentation to make sure she still meets criteria for admission. If she does, offer to reach out to the medical director of the insurance company to advocate on her behalf stating the benefits of an inpatient rehab stay (multidisciplinary, intensive therapies, and medical oversight). You may highlight potential long-term cost savings with less morbidity and reduced rates of readmissions for patients receiving intensive therapies before going home after a prolonged hospitalization. Provide additional written justification and supplemental information to the insurance company to support your recommendation.

5. You learn that the patient will not admit because of an insurance denial. She will be going home with family and she is really upset and fearful of going home. How would you approach this situation?

First, share partnership in the recovery process and remind the patient of things learned in the first stay at rehab. Empower her by giving her a clear and concise plan for home health or outpatient therapy and give clear directions for discharge follow up. Empathize with her about her feelings and frustrations; validate them but also refocus her to what can still be accomplished. Remember that this disease can affect quality of life. The astute physician will fully explore the biopsychosocial barriers that concerns the patient.

She calls you in at your office and says she has been falling since being home. What would you ask the patient? How would you advise her?

First, ask her about any related injuries and context of the falls (i.e., environmental, polypharmacy, disease progression, neurological/cardiac). She says, "I mostly fall when using the stairs. My bedroom is on the 2nd floor. Oh, and I fell once in the bathroom after slipping in the shower". Make sure she received all her DME that was recommended during her rehab stay, especially the bath items, and that she knows how to safely use the items. It is essential to schedule her for an office visit as soon as possible and perform a physical examination. Ask her to explore options of staying downstairs to decrease use of the stairs unless supervised or assisted. You may also check on HEP compliance. You may consider sending her to outpatient physical therapy if you think she has unmet functional goals and include fall recovery and stair management in the prescription. Patients with several falls, especially the geriatric population, may benefit from medical alert emergency call systems. If a cause of falls is not clearly identified, you may recommend follow up with primary care or refer to specialists (neurology) for further work-up.

Notes: The most common tool used to identify extent of MS-related disability is the Expanded Disability Status Scale (EDSS). Validated functional assessment tools include the 6-minute walk test and Berg Balance Scale.

References:

Olek M, Narayan R, Frohman E, and Frohman T. Multiple sclerosis. https://uptodate.com.

Menon V, Saxena R, Misra R, and Phuljhele S. Management of optic neuritis. J Ophthalmol. 2011 Mar-Apr;59(2):117-22. doi: 10.4103/0301-4738.77020. PMID: 21350281; PMCID: PMC3116540.

Kurtzke JF. Disability rating scales in multiple sclerosis. Ann N Y Acad Sci. 1984;436:347-60. doi: 10.1111/j.1749-6632.1984.tb14805.x. PMID: 6598017.

Langdon DW and Thompson AJ. Multiple sclerosis: a preliminary study of selected variables affecting rehabilitation outcome. Multiple Sclerosis Journal. 1999;5(2):94-100. doi:10.1177/135245859900500205.

Kidd, D., et al. The benefit of inpatient neurorehabilitation in multiple sclerosis. Clinical rehabilitation. 1995;9(3):198-203.

Case: Hip Pain

A 40-year-old female presents to your outpatient clinic with a complaint of hip pain.

1. What history would you like to know?

The patient is a former competitive snowboarder that reports right posterior hip pain for the past 5 years, with worsening over the last 4 months. She points to the right sacroiliac joint region as the site of her pain. Her pain is constant, intermittently worse with prolonged standing, sitting and walking. She had radiation of pain and numbness to her posterior thigh when she sits for an extended period. She reports that she is doing her home exercise program for her core and back region which do little to change the pain. She does not recall any injuries in the past 4-5 months. However, she has had a long history of low back pain, after sustaining a snowboarding accident 5 years prior. She reports she has had multiple interventions for her low back pain. Including physical therapy, lumbar epidural steroids injections, facet joint injections, and eventually underwent laminectomy and fusion of her L4-S1 which resulted in improved right-sided leg pain.

2. What physical examination would you do?

Well healed lumbar laminectomy scar. No signs of atrophy to the lower extremities, abdominal and back region. Mild tenderness to the lumbar paraspinals and multifidi. Severe tenderness to the right sacroiliac joint. She has full active hip and knee range of motion. Lumbar range of motion with slight restriction in extension, otherwise is within normal limits. Lower extremity reflexes and sensation are intact. Right hip flexion is 4/5 due to pain otherwise her lower extremity strength is 5/5. Special testing is positive for FABER with pain at the right sacroiliac joint, positive for sacroiliac compression. Negative for Gaenslen's and sacroiliac distraction. Log roll, FAIR, Thomas, and Ober's are negative. Straight leg raise is negative.

3. Based on the history and physical exam findings, what is your differential diagnosis?

Sacroiliac joint pain, Piriformis syndrome, Gluteal bursitis, Gluteal strain, Lumbar radiculopathy, Lumbar stenosis, Iliotibial band syndrome, Greater trochanteric pain syndrome, Hip osteoarthritis, Ovarian Cysts, and Endometriosis.

4. What diagnostics would you order for this patient?

Sacroiliac joint XR for possible sacroiliac pathology, bilateral hip XR to examine possible hip pathology, lumbar XR to evaluate causes of referred pain. MRI lumbar consideration in high suspicion for radiculopathy or stenosis. Consider sacroiliac joint MRI in evaluation of sacroiliitis with concern for ankylosing spondylosis..

5. Assuming the diagnosis is right sacroiliac joint pain, what is your plan for management?

Physical therapy for targeted muscle stretching, core stability, muscle energy technique correction of asymmetry and motor control re-education of the hip and pelvis region. Sacroiliac joint belt bracing. Modalities, topical and oral medications consideration for symptomatic sacroiliac joint pain. Consider injections in refractory cases. However, advise that injections are only about 50 to 75% effective. If failure of all conservative options then minimally invasive sacroiliac joint fusion can be considered.

6. You find out 1 month after the right sacroiliac joint injection that there was a recall in the lot number of the corticosteroid that you used in the procedure. How would you respond to this situation?

Call the patient and advise her that there has been a recall issued for the medication that was used in the procedure. Evaluate for potential complications via telephone, in-person visit and possible referral for further work up depending on the situation. Consider lab work, imaging as appropriate. Work with the medication supplier, state and federal resources for reporting of potential adverse outcomes related to this medication.

7. Roleplaying the situation: The patient returns to your clinic reporting severe pain after her sacroiliac joint injection with you 4 days ago. How would you approach this situation?

Be empathetic that the patient did not have the outcome she desired with the procedure. Practice active listening and discuss her concerns. Reassess the patient considering reinjury, new injuries or possible complications from the procedure. Consider that there is often a delayed effect of pain with corticosteroid injections.

References:

Cibulka, M. T., & Koldehoff, R. (1999). Clinical usefulness of a cluster of sacroiliac joint tests in patients with and without low back pain. Journal of Orthopaedic & Sports Physical Therapy, 29(2), 83-92.

Richardson, C. A., Snijders, C. J., Hides, J. A., Damen, L., Pas, M. S., & Storm, J. (2002). The relation between the transversus abdominis muscles, sacroiliac joint mechanics, and low back pain. Spine, 27(4), 399-405.

Rashbaum, R. F., Ohnmeiss, D. D., Lindley, E. M., Kitchel, S. H., & Patel, V. V. (2016). Sacroiliac joint pain and its treatment. Journal of Spinal Disorders and Techniques, 29(2), 42-48.

DePalma, M. J., Ketchum, J. M., & Saullo, T. R. (2011). Etiology of chronic low back pain in patients having undergone lumbar fusion. Pain Medicine, 12(5), 732-739.

Polly, D. W., Swofford, J., Whang, P. G., Frank, C. J., Glaser, J. A., Limoni, R. P., ... & INSITE Study Group. (2016). Two-year outcomes from a randomized controlled trial of minimally invasive sacroiliac joint fusion vs. non-surgical management for sacroiliac joint dysfunction. International journal of spine surgery, 10.

Lambert, R. G., Bakker, P. A., van der Heijde, D., Weber, U., Rudwaleit, M., Hermann, K. G. A., ... & Landewé, R. (2016). Defining active sacroiliitis on MRI for classification of axial spondyloarthritis: update by the ASAS MRI working group. Annals of the rheumatic diseases, 75(11), 1958-1963.

Case: Cardiac Rehabilitation

A 58-year-old male presents to your clinic complaints of dizziness and fatigue following his acute hospital stay three months ago.

1. What history would you like to know?

The patient reports that he was hospitalized for six days for chest pain management. The discharge summary he provides shows that he was managed for NSTEMI. He has a long history of coronary artery disease, hyperlipidemia, and diabetes type II. His medications include aspirin, metoprolol, nitroglycerin, simvastatin, and metformin. He endorses subjective weakness with all his tasks and activities since his hospitalization. He reports decreased activity tolerance and reports he is only able to walk one block compared to three blocks that he was able to do prior. He denies any back, upper and lower extremity pain. He denies vertigo. He reports sometimes that he feels like he is going to "black out". He denies headaches. He reports he has a family history of heart disease. His brother had his first myocardial infarction at age 45.

2. What physical examination would you do?

Obtained vital signs, heart rate: 98, respiratory rate: 12, blood pressure 148/80, BMI 36. Orthostatic blood pressure negative. Bilateral lower extremity edema +1. No signs muscle atrophy, no scars. Auscultation of heart, with regular rate, regular rhythm, no murmurs. Auscultation of lungs clear, no crackles. Muscle strength testing 4+/5 all extremities. Deep tendon reflexes intact. Sensation intact to extremities. Cranial nerves II-XII intact.

3. Based on the history and physical exam findings, what is your differential diagnosis?

Generalized weakness, Congestive heart failure myopathy, Sarcopenia, Atrial fibrillation related syncope, Orthostatic hypotension, Polyneuropathy, Pneumonia, and Spinal stenosis.

4. What diagnostics would you order for this patient?

Chest XR to evaluate for possible cardiomegaly, pulmonary edema, and pneumonia. EKG for evaluation of heart arrhythmias. ECHO for evaluation of cardiac function. NCS/EMG if suspecting possible neuropathy/myopathy.

5. Assuming the diagnosis is generalized weakness following acute stay for NSTEMI, what is your plan for management?

Recommendation to follow up with cardiology for management of secondary prevention program. Physical therapy for generalized strengthening, conditioning, and focus on improving activity tolerance. Establishing a safe heart rate /activity level via cardiac stress testing.

6. Your patient reports that there are no certified cardiac rehabilitation physical therapists around where he lives. How would you approach the situation?

Consider referral to generalized physical therapy for general strength and condition for decondition with activity restrictions based on cardiac stress testing. Advise the patient on alternative ways to gauge their activity level including self-pulse checks, use of smart devices for cardiac heart rate and rhythm reports, the talk test, and the BORG scale. Consider calling therapists local to the patient to form a partnership regarding creation of an outpatient cardiac rehabilitation program.

7. Roleplaying the situation: He reports to your clinic discouraged about how he is unable to play recreational basketball the way that he was prior. As a result, he has noticed that when he does not take his beta-block that he is able to play for longer and feel more energized. How would you advise him?

Be empathetic. Practice active listening and discuss his concerns. Express empathy that he was unable to continue his regular recreational activities. Acknowledge his desire to be more functional. Advise him that his beta-blocker is part of his secondary prevention program and is important in the overall management of his risk. Advise that you can help him reach out to his cardiologist about alternative medications and medication adjustments. Emphasize that it is important to keep his healthcare team apprised of self-medication adjustments as it can affect his overall care.

References:

Mampuya, W. M. (2012). Cardiac rehabilitation past, present and future: an overview. Cardiovascular diagnosis and therapy, 2(1), 38.

Heran, B. S., Chen, J. M., Ebrahim, S., Moxham, T., Oldridge, N., Rees, K., ... & Taylor, R. S. (2011). Exercise-based cardiac rehabilitation for coronary heart disease. Cochrane database of systematic reviews, (7).

Menezes, A. R., Lavie, C. J., Milani, R. V., Forman, D. E., King, M., & Williams, M. A. (2014). Cardiac rehabilitation in the United States. Progress in cardiovascular diseases, 56(5), 522-529.

Case: Hand Weakness

A 26-year-old otherwise healthy right hand dominant female presents with right hand weakness worsening over the last 3 years.

1. What would you like to know on history and physical examination?

She is a PhD student and about 1-year ago noticed difficulty with typing accuracy because of right hand fatigue. This was soon followed by aching in her medial forearm and fifth digit with difficulty grasping objects. She has not noticed numbness and has occasional non-radiating neck pain since being diagnosed with "whiplash" 3 years ago and she does not have shoulder pain. She denies weakness on the left. Review of systems is negative for skin pallor or arm swelling. On examination skin is warm to touch and there is mild focal thenar atrophy. Reflexes are normal. Motor abnormalities are limited to abductor pollicis brevis (4+/5), first dorsal interosseous (5-/5), and extensor indices 5-/5. Sensation is decreased in the medial antebrachial cutaneous (MAC) and ulnar sensory distribution. Radial pulse and capillary refill are normal. Special testing is unremarkable including Adson's and Roos tests, tinnel's at the wrist and elbow, median nerve compression, and Phalen's. Spurling's is negative.

2. What is your differential diagnosis and what work up would you do?

A lower trunk brachial plexus lesion such as neurogenic TOS (nTOS) is highly likely based on the distribution of weakness involving the C8 myotome of multiple peripheral nerves (radial /ulnar/median).

A differential for asymmetric hand weakness can be organized by each level of the peripheral nervous system (i.e., anterior horn cell down to the peripheral nerve (PN)). Here, starting proximal to distal, motor neuron disease (ALS, monomelic amyotrophy), C8-T1 radiculopathy (HNP), lower trunk plexopathy (TOS, Pancoast tumor, cervical 1st rib), and PN: multifocal motor mononeuropathy, median neuropathy (carpal tunnel syndrome) and ulnar neuropathy (cubital tunnel or Guyon's canal). Other considerations are cervical myelopathy (congenital, traumatic) or chronic regional pain syndrome.

Some of these can be easily excluded such as ALS because of the presence of pain, also, absence of radicular pain and the peripheral distribution of her aching pain are against an intraspinal canal lesion or a peripheral mononeuropathy.

NCS/EMG will be the test of choice. Classic NCS/EMG findings are reduced amplitudes of the MAC and ulnar sensory (digit 5) and reduced amplitude in the median and ulnar (median more so than ulnar) motor responses with a normal median sensory response.

You may also get a chest and cervical X-ray (rudimentary cervical rib, elongated C7 transverse process). An ultrasound (venous) and CTA/MRA chest (arterial) should be chosen if vascular TOS is suspected.

3. The patient has electrodiagnostic confirmed nTOS. What is your rehabilitation plan?

Conservatively, first line treatment would include physical therapy (nerve glides, stretching, range of motion with attention to the scalene muscles), posture/ergonomic education, analgesics (NSAIDs, muscle relaxants), and injection therapy (steroids, botulinum toxin A; scalenes are usual target).

This patient has mild focal atrophy and weakness on examination and should be considered for surgical options if 4-6 weeks of conservative treatment is unsuccessful. nTOS is often associated with a taut congenital band that extends from an elongated C7 transverse process or cervical rib to the first thoracic rib injuring T1 nerve fibers more than C8. Surgery removes the congenital band and halts progression of weakness; however, atrophy is not reversed.

4. Briefly explain neurogenic and vascular TOS and the clinical presentation.

The common cause is compression of the brachial plexus and/or subclavian vessels in the thoracic outlet (interscalene triangle, costoclavicular space, retropectoralis minor space). The three main types are neurogenic (nTOS), arterial (aTOS), and venous (vTOS). Neurogenic is the most common manifestation representing about 95% of the cases with about 5% vascular. Rarely, in approximately 1% of cases, "true" nTOS is confirmed with abnormal electrodiagnostic studies. More commonly, "disputed" nTOS is the diagnosis of exclusion based on constellation of findings pain, paresthesia, and weakness and is sometimes precipitated by superimposed neck trauma. Disputed usually responds well to conservative care. Vascular is subdivided into arterial (aTOS) and venous (vTOS) with involvement of the subclavian vasculature presenting as deep pain in the arm, chest, shoulder, heaviness in the arm, skin pallor, or cyanosis.

5. Your patient returns after having surgery and wants more occupational hand therapy. She has had 24 visits and appears to have met all her functional goals. What would you say to the patient?

You: "Ms. Wright, can you tell me about what your goals are with additional therapy?" Ms Wright: "I still feel my grip is weak and they have this really neat machine that I use every time I go there. I also like the idea of having someone coach me through my exercises and keep me on task." You: "I see, well, I am looking at your therapy discharge notes, and I share with you good news that the therapist feels you are ready to transition to a HEP. Do you feel you can do your HEP? What are some of the barriers you are experiencing? You mentioned a machine, is this something you can get access to at a gym or purchase? When you said you like to have a coach to keep you on task, can you think of ways to do this at home?" Give examples such as scheduling routine HEP time, keeping a HEP diary, using technology/smart devices, or incorporating fun task-specific exercises so it is not "work". Ms. Wright: "These are great ideas. I think you are right; I can do my HEP. Can I call you if I have any setbacks or need help with my HEP?" You: "Absolutely! In fact, let's schedule a phone follow up visit in 6-weeks to see how you are doing." Ms. Wright: "Thank you!"

References:

Li N, Dierks G, Vervaeke HE, Jumonville A, Kaye AD, Myrcik D, Paladini A, Varrassi G, Viswanath O, and Urits I. Thoracic Outlet Syndrome: A Narrative Review. J Clin Med. 2021 Mar 1;10(5):962. doi: 10.3390/jcm10050962. PMID: 33804565; PMCID: PMC7957681.

Tsao B, Ferrante A., Wilbourn A, and Shields R. Electrodiagnostic features of true neurogenic thoracic outlet syndrome. Muscle Nerve. 2014;49:724-727. https://doi.org/10.1002/mus.24066

Huang J and Zager, EL. Thoracic Outlet Syndrome. *Neurosurgery.* Oct 2004;55(4):897-903. https://doi.org/10.1227/01.NEU.0000137333.04342.4D.

Fugate MW, Rotellini-Coltvet L, and Freischlag JA. Current management of thoracic outlet syndrome. Curr Treat Options Cardio Med. 2009;11(176). https://doi.org/10.1007/s11936-009-0018-4.

Kuhn J, Lebus G, and Bible J. Thoracic outlet syndrome. J of AAOS. April 2015;23(4):p222-232. doi: 10.5435/JAAOS-D-13-00215.

Case: Heel Pain

A 30-year-old male presents to your outpatient clinic with a complaint of heel pain.

1. What history would you like to know?

The patient is a professional basketball player. He reports that he has had left-sided heel pain on and off for the last 6 months. He does not recall any specific injury event. He has had several bad ankle sprains over the years and wears specialized braces and high-top basketball shoes when he plays and trains. He reports pain with initial push off and with both jumping and landing motions. His pain is improved with relative rest, ice, physical treatments, and topical gels.

2. What physical examination would you do?

No signs of atrophy to the lower extremities and bilateral pes planus. There is no swelling to the bilateral foot and ankle. There is tenderness with palpation to the left Achilles tendon region. He has full active range of motion to his lower extremities. Lower extremity strength, reflexes, and sensation are intact. Special testing anterior, posterior drawer of the ankle, and talar tilt test are negative. Thomson test is negative bilaterally. There is no knee or hip pain. Special testing is negative for both the knee and hip.

3. Based on the history and physical exam findings, what is your differential diagnosis?

Achilles tendonitis, Heel spurs, Ankle osteoarthritis, Calcaneal stress fracture, Heel pad syndrome, Achilles rupture, Ankle fracture, and Tarsal tunnel syndrome.

4. What diagnostics would you order for this patient?

Ankle and foot XR to evaluate alignment, fracture, predisposition of impingement, calcific tendonitis, consider knee and hip XR to rule out possible knee or hip pathology, in clinic ultrasound to evaluate possible soft tissues injury, and tendinopathy, consideration for MRI ankle/foot if refractory to treatment.

5. Assuming the diagnosis is Achilles tendonitis what is your plan for management?

Main treatment is physical therapy for correction of biomechanics, motor re-education, strengthening of the hip, gluteal, quadriceps, mobility of the ankle and foot, stepwise progression from closed chain exercise to open chain exercise, and isometric to isotonic to eccentric exercise. Medications including topicals, and NSAIDs. Consideration for relative rest from his sporting activity with gradual return to play as he becomes more pain free. He may benefit from orthotics given his pes planus. Consider prolotherapy injections and surgical referral for refractory cases.

6. The patient reports that the coverage for prolotherapy injections had been denied. How can you help advocate for him?

Offer to call his insurance company about the denial of the injections. Consider drafting an appeal letter to send to the insurance company. Consider including the evidence for prolotherapy in your appeal and request a peer to peer. Discuss alternatives including possible surgical referral since he has refractory pain and dysfunction.

7. Roleplaying the situation: The patient reports that he feels that the treatment plan is taking too long. As a result, he had dry needling procedure done by a new physical therapist, which unfortunately, resulted in more pain and new numbness and tingling. How would you manage this situation?

Be empathetic with the patient about what happened during the dry needling procedure. Screen for red flags including signs of myelopathy, infection, and fracture. If red flags are present, ask him to present to the emergency department for prompt reassessment. If he is stable, ask him to come into the clinic as soon as possible so that you can reassess him. Avoid blaming the physical therapist during the encounter. Avoid making or confirming references to possible causality of the dry needling procedure, as it is not appropriate with proper reassessment.

References:

Longo, U. G., Ronga, M., & Maffulli, N. (2018). Achilles tendinopathy. Sports medicine and arthroscopy review, 26(1), 16-30.

Hutchison AM, Evans R, Bodger O, Pallister I, Topliss C, Williams P, Vannet N, Morris V, Beard D. What is the best clinical test for Achilles tendinopathy?. Foot and ankle surgery. 2013 Jun 1;19(2):112-7.

Alfredson, H., & Cook, J. (2007). A treatment algorithm for managing Achilles tendinopathy: new treatment options. British journal of sports medicine, 41(4), 211-216.

Morath O, Kubosch EJ, Taeymans J, Zwingmann J, Konstantinidis L, Südkamp NP, Hirschmüller A. The effect of sclerotherapy and prolotherapy on chronic painful Achilles tendinopathy—a systematic review including meta-analysis. Scandinavian journal of medicine & science in sports. 2018 Jan;28(1):4-15.

Kim DC, Glenzer S, Johnson A, Nimityongskul P. Deep infection following dry needling in a young athlete: an underreported complication of an increasingly prevalent modality: a case report. JBJS case connector. 2018 Sep 1;8(3):e73.

Case: Deconditioning in a long-term skilled nursing facility

The director of rehabilitation at a local skilled nursing facility (SNF) places a consult for rehabilitation appropriateness for a 90-year-old male he has recently readmitted to the SNF after an acute hospital stay.

1. What history would you like to know?

He is a long-term resident of the SNF with a diagnosis of dementia. Three weeks ago, he suffered an unwitnessed fall and was transferred to the acute hospital for work up. He was found to have sepsis due to UTI and was started on antibiotics and transferred back to the facility after three days. Since returning, the nurses have noticed that he requires more assistance than before. It is reported at baseline that he is modified independent with a single point cane for ambulation and independent for ADLs. Nurses report that he does not seem as engaged compared to before his acute hospital stay. He is on medications for hypertension, hyperlipidemia, and coronary artery disease.

2. What physical examination would you do?

No skin lesions, ecchymosis, signs of trauma on inspection. He appears to have flat affect and masked faces. He has vertical gaze palsy, otherwise unremarkable cranial nerve exam. There is a positive glabellar sign. He has full strength with extremity testing and range of motion is within normal limits but noted mild rigidity. He has trouble with initiation of movements on your exam. The has signs of pill rolling and a shuffling gait.

3. Based on the history and physical exam findings, what is your differential diagnosis?

Parkinson disease, Drug-induced Parkinsonism, Depression, Pseudo-dementia, Stroke, Generalized Weakness, Sarcopenia, and Infectious disease process.

4. What diagnostics would you order for this patient?

Urinary analysis, CBC and CMP to rule out infection and metabolic causes for change in function. Consider brain imaging if suspicious for other intracranial processes.

5. Assuming the diagnosis is Parkinson's disease, what is your plan for management?

Review his medication list to rule out patient medications that may contribute or worsen parkinsonism. Referral to neurology for possible initiation of Carbidopa, Levodopa. Depending on functional level he may need both physical and occupational therapy. Evaluation by physical therapy and occupational therapy for functional level, equipment needs. Consider specialized Parkinson's therapy, gait training, and transfer training.

6. The SNF provides you with a denial of coverage for the requested physical therapy due to medical necessity. How would you advocate for this patient?

Review the denial claim and the documentation that was sent for authorization. Draft an appeal and consider contacting the insurance company to do a peer to peer. Consider that he has a new diagnosis of Parkinson's disease with specific impairments that can be used as a part of an appeal to justify medical necessity of therapy.

7. Roleplaying the situation: The director of rehabilitation does not have therapists that are certified in specialized Parkinson's therapy on his team. He appears annoyed at the order for such therapy. How would you diffuse the situation?

Be empathetic and acknowledge the concerns for the need for specific training for specialized Parkinson's therapy. Work with the director of rehabilitation and the therapists as a team to find specific exercises, and interventions that work within the skilled nursing facilities operations.

References:

Medicare Benefit Policy Manual. Chapter 8 - Coverage of Extended Care (SNF) Services. Under Hospital Insurance

Abbruzzese, G., Marchese, R., Avanzino, L., & Pelosin, E. (2016). Rehabilitation for Parkinson's disease: Current outlook and future challenges. Parkinsonism & related disorders, 22, S60-S64.

McDonnell, M. N., Rischbieth, B., Schammer, T. T., Seaforth, C., Shaw, A. J., & Phillips, A. C. (2018). Lee Silverman Voice Treatment (LSVT)-BIG to improve motor function in people with Parkinson's disease: a systematic review and meta-analysis. Clinical rehabilitation, 32(5), 607-618.

Case: Pelvic pain

A 46-year-old female presents to your outpatient clinic with a complaint of chronic right sided hip pain.

1. What history would you like to know?

The patient reports she has had right-sided hip and groin pain for 12 years since the birth of her first child. She reports gradual increase in frequency in pain and now has experienced constant pain for the last 5 years. She reports a deep ache sensation in the right groin. It is made worse with attempting to lift objects and bending over. She reports axial back pain for about 10 years. No bowel and no bladder incontinence. She does not recall any injuries in the past. She has intermittently used Ibuprofen and Tylenol without much relief in the past. She had a course of physical therapy for her back 3 years ago and did not feel that she benefited from it.

2. Which physical examinations would you do?

With a chaperone present, physical examination reveals tenderness to palpation to the pelvic floor muscles (levator ani, coccygeus). Tenderness to palpation to the ischial tuberosity on the right, and right round ligament. Nontender lower back region. Normal strength and reflexes to the lower extremities. Special testing: Positive SI joint compression test. No Fortin finger sign. Negative FABER, SI joint distraction test, and Gaenslen's Test. Negative FAIR test, hip Scour test, and Log roll test. Lumbar special testing is negative. No hernia is identified.

3. Based on the history and physical exam findings, what is your differential diagnosis?

Pelvic floor dysfunction, Sacroiliitis, Sacroiliac Joint Pain, Coccydynia, Hernia, Myofascial pain, Hamstring strain, Lumbar radiculopathy, Hip osteoarthritis, Femoral acetabular impingement syndrome, Endometriosis, Ovarian cysts.

4. What diagnostics would you order for this patient?

Pelvis and bilateral hip XR for possible hip pathology. Sacroiliac and Coccyx XR for sacroiliac and coccyx pathology. Lumbar XR for possible spine pathology. MRI lumbar spine if suspecting intraspinal canal pathology, or radiculopathy. Abdominal ultrasound for liver, and gallbladder pathology.

5. Assuming the diagnosis is pelvic floor dysfunction, what is your plan for management?

Physical therapy for pelvic rehabilitation, core strength, and hip mechanics. Consideration for biofeedback and cognitive behavioral therapy. Medications including NSAIDs, neuropathics, and antidepressants. Further work-up including advanced imaging, and consultation to other services including General Surgery, and/or Obstetrics & Gynecology for recommendations in refractory cases.

6. Your patient reports that she has been able to have less pain and feel more functional since she has been seeing her acupuncturist twice a month. However, her insurance is no longer approving additional sessions. How would respond to this?

Document the pain and functional improvements that your patient is reporting. Offer to help her with the appeal process for more potential sessions. Consider requesting a peer to peer with the insurance company to make her case. Consider offering referral for the patient to alternative adjuvant treatments such as chiropractic, osteopathic manipulative treatment, cognitive behavioral therapy, and/or biofeedback.

7. Roleplaying the situation: The patient returns to your clinic for follow up reporting increased pain since her acupuncture sessions have ended. She is requesting stronger medications, as the ibuprofen no longer "cuts it" and wants a prescription for oxycodone. How would you respond?

Be empathetic. Practice active listening and revisit her concerns. Express empathy that she was unable to continue a treatment that was helping her and acknowledge her desire to be more functional and in less pain. Advise her that opioids are typically not indicated for management of her condition and consider prescribing alternatives, such as neuropathics and/or antidepressants. Consider referral to a second opinion regarding opioids if she continues to want the medication despite your efforts at education.

References:

Harvey, M. A. (2003). Pelvic floor exercises during and after pregnancy: a systematic review of their role in preventing pelvic floor dysfunction. Journal of Obstetrics and Gynaecology Canada, 25(6), 487-498.

Prather, H., Spitznagle, T. M., & Dugan, S. A. (2007). Recognizing and treating pelvic pain and pelvic floor dysfunction. Physical medicine and rehabilitation clinics of North America, 18(3), 477-496.

Urits, I., Callan, J., Moore, W. C., Fuller, M. C., Renschler, J. S., Fisher, P., ... & Viswanath, O. (2020). Cognitive behavioral therapy for the treatment of chronic pelvic pain. Best Practice & Research Clinical Anaesthesiology.

Newman, D. K. (2014). Pelvic floor muscle rehabilitation using biofeedback. Urol Nurs, 34(4), 193-202.

Walker, E. A., Sullivan, M. D., & Stenchever, M. A. (1993). Use of antidepressants in the management of women with chronic pelvic pain. Obstetrics and gynecology clinics of North America, 20(4), 743-751.

Case: Stroke

A 46-year-old female presents to inpatient rehabilitation after an MCA stroke.

1. What history would you like to know?

The patient is dysarthric but family at the bed-side reports she has had a stroke 5 days ago with sudden onset of slurred speech and weakness. She received thrombolytic therapy and was monitored and treated at the hospital. She has had high blood pressure and diabetes for the last 5 years. She lives with her family. She has 2 children 10-years-old and 15-years-old. She lives in a 1 story house and was independent prior to the stroke.

2. What physical examination would you do?

Physical examination reveals left flaccid hemiplegia, left sided fascial droop, dysarthria and left-hemineglect. Reflexes are 0+ on the left and 1+ on the right. Sensation is intact.

3. Overnight, you are called to the bedside for worsening symptoms and unresponsiveness. What is your differential diagnosis?

Urinary tract infection, hemorrhagic conversation, cerebral edema, uncal herniation

4. What diagnostics would you order for this patient?

STAT CT, urine analysis with reflex culture, CBC, BMP, PT/INR, Blood culture, lactic acid.

5. Assuming the diagnosis is hemorrhagic conversion what is your plan for management?

Immediate transfer to acute service for medical monitoring including cardiovascular and respiratory management, monitoring for neurological deterioration, treatment of elevated intracranial pressure and seizures.

6. Roleplaying the situation: Your patient returns to acute inpatient rehabilitation a week later. The family is upset and wants to know what happened. How would you respond?

Be empathetic. Express that the patient had a severe decline in status from a hemorrhagic conversion. Review the risks of hemorrhagic conversion with the family. Review the CT scan findings with the family. Advise the family on plans in inpatient rehabilitation to help the patient recover.

References:

Yaghi, S., Willey, J. Z., Cucchiara, B., Goldstein, J. N., Gonzales, N. R., Khatri, P., Kim, L. J., Mayer, S. A., Sheth, K. N., Schwamm, L. H., & American Heart Association Stroke Council; Council on Cardiovascular and Stroke Nursing; Council on Clinical Cardiology; and Council on Quality of Care and Outcomes Research (2017). Treatment and Outcome of Hemorrhagic Transformation After Intravenous Alteplase in Acute Ischemic Stroke: A Scientific Statement for Healthcare Professionals From the American Heart Association/American Stroke Association. Stroke, 48(12), e343–e361.

Spronk, E., Sykes, G., Falcione, S., Munsterman, D., Joy, T., Kamtchum-Tatuene, J., & Jickling, G. C. (2021). Hemorrhagic Transformation in Ischemic Stroke and the Role of Inflammation. Frontiers in neurology, 12, 661955. https://doi.org/10.3389/fneur.2021.661955

Case: Neck Pain

A 46-year-old female presents to your outpatient clinic with a complaint of chronic neck pain.

1. What history would you like to know?

The patient reports she has had neck pain for 12 years. She reports gradual increase in frequency in pain and now has experienced constant neck pain and headaches for the last 5 years. She reports a deep ache sensation in the upper neck area. It is made worse with twisting and bending her neck. She reports axial low back pain for about 10 years. No bowel and no bladder incontinence. She does not recall any injuries in the past. She has intermittently used Ibuprofen and Tylenol without much relief in the past. She has Rheumatoid Arthritis and is on DMARDS. She had a course of physical therapy for her neck 10 years ago and did not feel that she benefited from it.

2. What physical examination would you do?

Physical examination reveals tenderness to palpation to the paraspinal and occipital muscles. Patient has decreased strength in her hands and increased reflexes in the lower extremities. Patient has decreased rapid alternating motion in the fingers. Special testing: Positive Spurling's maneuver.

3. Based on the history and physical exam findings what is your differential diagnosis?

Cervical radiculopathy, atlanto axial instability, central cord syndrome, myofascial pain syndrome, cervical myelopathy

4. What diagnostics would you order for this patient?

Cervical XR and MRI for spine pathology in the setting of decreased fine motor, weakness, and hyperreflexia.

5. Assuming there is atlanto-axial instability what is your plan for management?

Immediate referral to Ortho Spine or Neurosurgery for evaluation of surgical fusion. Medications including NSAIDs and neuropathic agents.

6. Roleplaying the situation: Your patient reports that she does not want spine fusion and wants to use natural and conservative interventions for her neck. How would respond to this?

Be empathetic; practice active listen and review her concerns. Express empathy that she is scared and worried about the repercussions of an invasive surgery. Review the cervical MRI with her and the pathophysiology of atlanto-axial instability with her. Prescribing alternatives such as neuropathics, antidepressants, and acupuncture while she awaits surgical consideration. Consider referral to a 2nd opinion regarding surgery if she continues to want to pursue conservative treatment despite your counseling.

References:

Sorimachi, Y., Iizuka, H., Ara, T., Nishinome, M., Iizuka, Y., Nakajima, T., & Takagishi, K. (2011). Atlanto-axial joint of atlanto-axial subluxation patients due to rheumatoid arthritis before and after surgery: morphological evaluation using CT reconstruction. *European spine journal : official publication of the European Spine Society, the European Spinal Deformity Society, and the European Section of the Cervical Spine Research Society*, *20*(5), 798–803.

Drosos, A. A., Pelechas, E., Georgiadis, A. N., & Voulgari, P. V. (2021). A not-to-miss Cause of Severe Cervical Spine Pain in a Patient with Rheumatoid Arthritis: A Case-Based Review. Mediterranean journal of rheumatology, 32(3), 256–263. https://doi.org/10.31138/mjr.32.3.256

ADVANCED CASES

A. Cerebral Vascular Disease
B. CNS
C. Medical Conditions
D. MSK: Occupational Med / Sports
E. MSK Disorders
F. Neuromuscular Disorders
G. Spinal Cord Injury
H. TBI
I. Neurorehabilitation
J. Wrist Drop
K. Cervical Dystonia
L. Weakness
M. Mid Back Pain
N. Neck Pain
O. Breast Cancer

Case: Stroke

1. A 61-years-old male presents to your rehabilitation clinic with sudden dizziness, nausea, vomiting, weakness, and trouble speaking. What would you like to find out on history and physical examination?

2. The patient has had dizziness and blurry vision for the last hour. He has dysarthria and drooling. He has a medical history of hypertension and has a 30-packs per year smoking history. Upon physical examination his strength is 3/5 throughout the left side. Reflexes are 0+ throughout the left side. The patient has a left-sided facial droop and tongue deviation to the left. Blood pressure is 220/120. What is your differential diagnosis for this patient?

3. The most likely differentials are embolic stroke, hemorrhagic stroke, and cerebral aneurysm. Other differentials may include cluster headache, tension headache, occipital neuralgia, cerebral AVM, Moyamoya disease, amyloid angiopathy, abscess, tumor, and encephalopathy/infection.

Advanced Concepts for Differential Diagnosis:

- Thrombotic – Thrombotic strokes tend to occur at night with slow onset of symptoms.
- Embolic – Embolic strokes tend to occur during the day, are sudden and cardiogenic, and tend to affect the superior division of MCA.
- Lacunar infarcts – Lacunar infarcts occur in the small vessel and are present in long standing hypertension.
- Intracerebral hemorrhage - Patients tend to have a history of uncontrolled hypertension and appear calm on

presentation. ICH typically affects the putamen.

- Subarachnoid hemorrhage - SAH typically occurs during strenuous activity with sudden onset. SAH affect the anterior Circle of Willis.

- Superior division of MCA - Strokes in this location affect sensory and motor deficits on contralateral face and arm > leg. There also may be Broca's aphasia.

- Inferior division of MCA - Strokes in this area on the left hemisphere will cause Wernicke's aphasia. Strokes in this area in the right hemisphere will cause left visual neglect.

- ACA - Strokes affecting the ACA will result in contralateral weakness and sensory loss affecting mainly the distal contralateral leg (foot/ leg more affected than thigh). There may be urinary incontinence with contralateral grasp reflex and paratonic rigidity (Gegenhalten).

- Posterior cerebral artery - There may be visual field cuts when bilateral PCA are affected with a denial of cortical blindness (Anton syndrome). Weber syndrome results when there is oculomotor palsy with contralateral hemiplegia. Trochlear nerve palsy (vertical gaze palsy) may also result from PCA infarcts.

- Vertebrobasilar - Strokes in this area may result in Lateral Wallenberg Syndrome with ipsilateral Horner's, hiccups, contralateral pain, and temperature changes.

- Basilar artery - Strokes in this area may result in Locked in Syndrome where the patient is unable to move, but has full cognition.

What kind of work up do you initiate?

4. Work up should include STAT non-contrast CT, INR, and platelet count. A key intervention for embolic stroke is the restoration of blood flow to the brain with tPA within 4.5 hours. Other work up may include EKG, carotid ultrasound, MRI, echocardiogram, CBC, CMP, coagulation studies, cardiac biomarkers, toxicology screening, lipid profile, ANA, RPR, homocysteine level, RF, and ESR, particularly after tPA for continued work up of etiology of stroke. CBC, CMP, ESR, CRP, serum protein electrophoresis, RF, ANA, TSH. Skull x-ray may be considered if there is trauma. Cerebral angiography and transcranial Doppler may be considered for AVM and angiopathy.

Advanced Concepts for Work Up:
- CT scan – Acute bleeds show up bright.
- MRI is best used to find lacunar infarcts.
- MRI DWI is used to assess for penumbra.
- Carotid Ultrasound showing 70% carotid stenosis with unilateral symptoms should undergo carotid endarterectomy.
- Echocardiograms may show thrombosis or patent foramen ovale.
- Blood sugar – Keep Blood sugar <300.
- Lipid levels - statin, hypercoagulability labs - homocysteine

5. MRI shows a large right MCA infarct with developing cerebral edema. The patient is treated acutely in the hospital and is now medically ready for inpatient rehabilitation. What is your comprehensive treatment plan?

6. Comprehensive treatment plan should include nursing considerations (bowel/bladder management, Lovenox bridge for anticoagulation). The physician should be actively managing blood pressure medications and working with Neurology. PT should be involved for ambulation, strengthening, equipment needs. OT should be involved in ADL's and adaptive equipment. Speech should be involved for swallowing, dysarthria, and cognition. Social Work should be involved in social reintegration. The Case Manager should be actively working with the family on support systems for getting the patient back home.

7. The patient is discharged back home after inpatient rehabilitation. Soon thereafter, the family brings the patient in and is upset that his in-home physical therapy has been declined by the insurance plan. The son is extremely upset. What do you say to the patient's son?

Mr. Smith, I can see you are very upset. Can you tell me a little bit more to help me understand what you are feeling? ("I'm worried about my dad. He used to be so active. I'm worried that he'll die if we don't get him moving.") Mr. Smith, I can respect what you're feeling. A stroke is a difficult thing to deal with. ("Yes, it is. I'm just so worried.") I am committed to working with you and your father as a team. Let's get him into outpatient physical therapy while we work on getting your father more in-home support. Let's get some additional family support. I'd like to meet with you and your father in a week as a team to see how we can help your father get to a more functional level. ("Yes, that would be nice. Thank you so much, doctor."

References:

Gabriel, V., Holavanahalli, R., & Braddom, R. (2011). *Physical Medicine & Rehabilitation.* Philadelphia: Elsevier Saunders.

NICE Clinical Guidelines, No. 68. (2008) Stroke: National Clinical Guideline for Diagnosis and Initial Management of Acute Stroke and Transient Ischaemic Attack (TIA). National Collaborating Centre for Chronic Conditions (UK). London: Royal College of Physicians (UK).

Swedish Council on Health Technology Assessment. (2015). Rehabilitation at Home After Early Supported Discharge (ESD) for Elderly Patients After Stroke: Summary and conclusions SBU Yellow Report No. 234

Case: CNS

1. A 70-years-old male presents to your rehabilitation clinic with slowed movements, falls, tremor, and coordination difficulty. What history and physical examination findings would you like to know?

2. The wife reports that the patient has had frequent falls over the last 3 years along with worsening memory. There is no family history of dementia. He is slow to get up and walks with broad-based gait. He has a resting tremor and incontinence. He is unable to perform rapid alternating movement and scores 20/30 on the mini mental status exam. His strength and sensation are fully intact. Vital signs are normal. Speech is normal. Cranial nerves are intact. What is your differential diagnosis for this patient?

3. The most likely differentials are Parkinsonism, cerebellar stroke, cerebellar brain tumors, normal pressure hydrocephalus. Other differentials may include non-hereditary degenerative ataxia, ALS, alcohol use, toxins, and infections.

Advanced Concepts for Differential Diagnosis:

- Cerebellar tumor - cerebellar tremor 3Hz, mainly in a horizontal plane, most prominent with fine repetitive action of the extremities, and other signs of cerebellar ataxia.

- Drug-induced parkinsonism - Exposure to drugs such as haloperidol, metoclopramide, reserpine, amiodarone, and lithium

- Toxin-induced parkinsonism - manganese and carbon

monoxide

- Dementia pugilistica (post traumatic parkinsonism) - parkinsonism associated with repeated trauma to the head
- Parkinson disease with dementia - memory loss, fluctuating cognition, and visual hallucinations with motor features.
- Parkinson's – pill rolling tremor more prominent at rest with a 4-5Hz frequency, bradykinesia, cogwheel rigidity, festination, and postural instability
- Parkinson-plus syndromes - signs of parkinsonism plus additional signs of neurodegenerative lesions, and poorly responsive to levodopa therapy with overall worse prognosis than PD
- Progressive supranuclear palsy - vertical gaze palsy, Parkinsonian features with bradykinesia and rigidity
- Shy-Drager syndrome (progressive autonomic failure) - Parkinsonian features with autonomic dysfunction
- Olivopontocerebellar atrophy - Parkinsonian features with ataxia and dysarthria
- Striatonigral degeneration - Parkinsonian features with dystonia (anterocollis), and tremor uncommon
- Friedreich's ataxia – young child, mental retardation, and hyperreflexia
- Dentatorubral pallidoluysian atrophy - Japanese descent with family history
- Essential tremor - more prominent with activity (5-8Hz), diminished at rest, and also stress exacerbates the tremor
- Alcohol, drugs - physiologic tremor high-frequency tremor that is most prominent with posture and action, exacerbated by anxiety, and fatigue
- Frontotemporal dementia - overuse of stock phrases, lack of conversational initiation and echolalia
- Alzheimer disease - memory and visuospatial loss of function, and speech is more fluent than in persons with

> frontotemporal dementia.
> - Lewy body – hallucinations, and fluctuation
> - Vascular dementia - history of stroke or have focal neurologic deficits, early gait disturbance, changes in personality and mood, and also a history of frequent falls or unsteadiness

What kind of work up do you initiate?

4. Work up should include head CT, MRI, psychological screen, CMP, CBC, and UA. Other work up may include toxin screen, ESR, and CRP.

> **Advanced Concepts for Work Up:**
> - CT scan – Acute bleeds show up bright.
> - MRI is best used to find lacunar infarcts.
> - MRI DWI is used to assess for penumbra.
> - Carotid Ultrasound showing 70% carotid stenosis with unilateral symptoms should undergo carotid endarterectomy.
> - Echocardiograms may show thrombosis or patent foramen ovale.
> - Blood sugar – Keep blood sugar <300.
> - Lipid levels - statin, hypercoagulability labs - homocysteine

MRI of the brain is normal. There is no infection. You suspect Parkinson's disease with dementia. You refer the patient to a Neurologist who confirms the diagnosis. The patient sees you for follow up. What is your rehabilitation treatment plan?

5. Comprehensive treatment plan should include nursing considerations (bowel/bladder management). The physician should be actively working with Neurology on medication titration. PT should be involved for gait, falls and equipment such as a walker, and potentially "BIG" style-therapy. OT should be involved in ADL's and adaptive equipment like weight assisted utensils. Speech should be involved for swallowing and cognition. Patient should be placed in "Loud" therapy. Social Work should be involving the patient and family in local support groups.

6. The patient is doing well until a week ago when he began to wander away from home at night. The son is extremely upset. What do you say to the patient's son?

Mr. Smith, I can see you are very distressed. Can you tell me a little bit more to help me understand what you are feeling? ("I'm worried about my dad. I'm so tired and can't keep up at night. The police keep bringing my dad back home and I'm worried for his safety.") Mr. Smith, I can respect what you're feeling. This is an extremely difficult situation. ("Yes, it is. I'm just so overwhelmed.") I am committed to working with you and your father as a team. Let's get him into facility while we work on getting your father more in-home support. Let's get some additional family support. I'd like to meet with you and your family in a week as a team to see how we can help you and your father get more support and safety at home. I'll also call your Neurologist to see if there are additional medication changes that may help him. ("Yes, that would be nice. Thank you so much, doctor".)

References:

Gabriel, V., Holavanahalli, R., & Braddom, R. (2011). *Physical Medicine & Rehabilitation*. Philadelphia: Elsevier Saunders.

Hayashi A. (2013). Update rehabilitation therapy for Parkinson disease. Rinsho Shinkeigaku. 53(11):1046-9. Review. Japanese.

Synofzik M, Ilg W. (2014) Motor training in degenerative spinocerebellar disease: ataxia-specific improvements by intensive physiotherapy and exergames. Biomed Res Int. 2014:583507. doi: 10.1155/2014/583507. Epub 2014 Apr 27. Review.

Foster ER. (2014). Themes from the special issue on neurodegenerative diseases: what have we learned, and where can we go from here? Am J Occup Ther. Jan-Feb;68(1):6-8. doi: 10.5014/ajot.2014.009910.

Case: Medical Conditions

1. A 50-years-old female presents to your outpatient clinic with numbness and tingling in both of her hands and feet. What history and physical examination findings would you like to know?

2. There has been burning sensations in her legs for the past 12 months. She denies bowel or bladder problems. She denies any recent travel or exposure to toxins. Symptoms are progressively worsening. The patient has a broad-based gait on exam. Her strength is fully intact. Her sensation to light touch is decreased up to mid thigh and up to both wrists. Vital signs are normal. Speech is normal. Cranial nerves are intact. Lungs are clear to auscultation and heart sounds are normal. What is your differential diagnosis for this patient?

3. The most likely differentials are polyneuropathy, paraneoplastic syndrome, and diabetic neuropathy. Other differentials include hypothyroid, Lyme disease, lymphoma, monoclonal gammopathy, syphilis, vitamin B6 deficiency, vitamin B12 deficiency, cervical myelopathy, alcohol induced neuropathy, Charcot Marie Tooth, idiopathic polyneuropathy, CIDP, AIDP, and mononeuritis multiplex.

Advanced Concepts for Differential Diagnosis:

- COPD – smoking history, PFTs
- Pneumonia – responds to antibiotics
- Family antitrypsin deficiency
- Polyneuropathy refers to pathology affecting multiple peripheral nerves and involves the cell body, axon, myelin sheath, or a combination of the above.
- Barohn and Amato 3-6-10 approach to neuropathy - 3 Goals: Determine anatomical and physiological locations, and treatment. 6 Questions: systems, distribution, nature, upper motor neuron, temporality, hereditary. 10 Phenotypic Patterns - see references
- Asymmetric proprioceptive sensory loss without weakness - cancer, paraneoplastic syndromes (small cell lung cancer, lymphoma, multiple myeloma, others, Sjögren's syndrome, idiopathic sensory neuronopathy, cisplatinum, vitamin B6 toxicity, and HIV-related sensory neuronopathy

What kind of work up do you initiate?

4. Work up should include CBC, CMP, ESR, fasting blood glucose, vitamin B12, TSH, HIV, HBA1C, ANA, UA serum protein electrophoresis, urine protein electrophoresis, RPR, hepatitis panel, EMG/NCS, and chest x-ray.

Advanced Concepts for Work Up:

- Highest yield: Fasting blood sugar - if negative then glucose tolerance test, Serum B12 with metabolites (methymalonic acid with/without homocysteine), SPEP with immunofixation, UPEP, +/- quantitative immunoglobulins

- If Axon Loss, consider: ESR, CRP, Rheumatoid factor (RF), Antinuclear antibody (ANA), TSH with reflex T4, CBC with differential, complete metabolic panel, and serum folate

- Suspected Demyelinating/ Neuropathy Polyneuropathy - RF, anti-cyclic citrullinated peptide (anti-CCP) antibody, ANA panel (anti-dsDNA, anti-Sm, SS-A (Ro), SS-B (La), anti-RNP, anti-Jo, anti-centromere, Scl-70, others as indicated), Anticytoplasmic antibodies: p-ANCA, c-ANCA, Cryoglobulins, Serum complement, and Lyme titer

- Infections: Campylobacter jejuni, Hepatitis, HIV, RPR, and CMV

- Heavy metals from serum and/or 24-hour urine

- Paraneoplastic panel (anti-Hu)

- Autoantibodies: - Anti-MAG, anti-sulfatide (neuropathies associated with paraproteinemia), Anti-GM1 (Multifocal motor neuropathy, AMAN), and Anti-GQ1b (Miller-Fisher syndrome)

- Genetic testing CMT 1A (PMP22 duplication), HNPP (PMP22 deletion), X-linked CMT (connexin-32), and CMT 2A (mitofusin 2)

Chest x-ray shows a mass. EMG/NCS findings were consistent with sensorimotor peripheral neuropathy. You refer the patient to an Oncologist for work up and the patient is diagnosed with lung cancer. The patient follows up with you for cancer rehabilitation. What is your rehabilitation treatment plan?

5. Comprehensive treatment plan should include nursing considerations particularly dietary interventions. The physician should be actively working with the Oncologist with symptom monitoring when starting chemotherapy or radiation therapy. PT may be involved with gait, balance, and equipment such as a walker. OT should be involved in ADL's and adaptive equipment if needed. Speech should be involved for swallowing particularly for oral cancers. Social Work should be involving the patient and family in local support groups. The patient should be involved in maximizing cardiovascular exercise prior to cancer treatment and continuing cardiovascular exercise throughout treatment.

The patient was doing well until a week ago when she began to lose large amounts of weight and experience severe fatigue. The son is extremely upset. What do you say to the patient's son?

6. Mr. Smith, I can see you are very distressed. Can you tell me a little bit more to help me understand what you are feeling? ("I'm worried about my mother. She keeps dropping weight and is so tired. She keeps saying she's going to die.") Mr. Smith, I can respect what you're feeling. This is an extremely difficult situation. ("Yes, it is. I'm not ready to lose my mother.") I am committed to working with you and your mother as a team. Let's get some additional family support. I'd also like to add some additional oral supplements and appetite stimulants. I'll also call your Oncologist to see if there are additional labs we need to run. Let's set up another appointment in a few days to touch base. ("Yes, that would be nice. Thank you so much, doctor.")

References:

Gabriel, V., Holavanahalli, R., & Braddom, R. (2011). *Physical Medicine & Rehabilitation*. Philadelphia: Elsevier Saunders.

Arnold ML (2013). Peripheral Neuropathy: Evaluation and differential diagnosis. PM&R Knowledge Now. https://now.aapmr.org/approach-to-peripheral-polyneuropathy-evaluation-and-differential-diagnosis/

Barohn, R. J., & Amato, A. A. (2013). Pattern-Recognition Approach to Neuropathy and Neuronopathy. Neurologic Clinics, 31(2), 343–361. https://doi.org/10.1016/j.ncl.2013.02.001

Case: MSK: Occupational Medicine

1. A 30-years-old male presents to your office with pain in the right leg for the past 4 weeks. What history and physical examination would you like to know?

2. The pain has been present for 4 weeks without any numbness. There is shooting pain down his leg and he cannot sit. He lifts heavy objects in a warehouse at work. He denies any acute trauma. On examination his strength and sensation are fully intact. Reflexes are normal. Straight leg raise is positive. What is your differential diagnosis for this patient?

3. The most likely differentials are lumbar disc herniation, radiculopathy, fracture, and ligament sprain. Other differentials include cancer, rheumatologic disease, peripheral nerve lesion, infection, and kidney stone.

> **Advanced Concepts for Differential Diagnosis:**
> - Renal Stones - radiating pain to anterior hip
> - Factures - Compression fracture, and trauma
> - Hamstring strain/tear
> - Osteosarcoma - worse night time pain, and pain out of proportion to presentation
> - Peripheral neuropathy - diabetics
> - Meralgia Paresthetica - overweight, wearing tight pants
> - Lower limb osteoarthritis - older individual
> - Femoral acetabular labral tear - anterior hip pain

What kind of work up do you initiate?

4. Work up should include x-ray of L-spine. You can consider a MRI. If nerve involvement is suspected, an EMG/NCS can be done. If systemic involvement is suspected, lab work should be initiated. Comprehensive evaluation may include a CBC with differential, ESR, CRP. These tests are useful when infection or malignancy is suspected.

> **Advanced Concepts for Work Up:**
> - Indications for x-ray: recent steroid use, trauma, neurologic deficit, alcohol use, drug use, constitutional symptoms, and prior cancer

5. X-ray is normal. What is your rehabilitation treatment plan including issues related to his work?

6. The physician should be actively considering pain management medications including topical medications and oral NSAIDS. PT should be prescribed. The patient should continue cardiovascular exercise. Patient should be placed on modified work duties. This is a good time to consider dietary counseling as well if the patient is open to it.

The patient follows up with you in 4 weeks and is extremely upset. He states that he cannot get better because you won't put him off work. How do you respond?

7. Mr. Smith, I can see you are very distressed. Can you tell me a little bit more to help me understand what you are feeling? ("I'm worried my job. If I don't rest, I won't get better and my job will let me go.") Mr. Smith, I can respect what you're feeling. This is an extremely difficult situation. ("Yes, it is. I want to get better.") I am committed to working with you and getting you back to work. Let's switch your medication. I'll also call your employer to see if we can get you a position that allows you to avoid heavy lifting and for you to change positions often. I'll also call your physical therapist to see what else we can do therapy wise. Let's set up another appointment in a few days to touch base. ("Yes, that would be nice. Thank you so much, doctor.")

References:

Patel AT, Ogle AA. (2000). Diagnosis and Management of Acute Low Back Pain. *Am Fam Physician*. Mar 15;61(6):1779-1786.

DeFronda SF, Daniels AH, Deren ME. (Differentiating Radiculopathy from Lower Extremity Arthropathy. *The American Journal of Medicine*. October. Volume 129, Issue 10, Pages 1124.e1–1124.e7https://doi.org/10.1016/j.amjmed.2016.06.019

Case: MSK Disorders

1. A 45-years-old male presents to your office with right calf pain that is worse with ambulation, but better with rest. What history and physical examination would you like to know?

2. The patient has a history of hypertension, diabetes, and has been smoking 1 pack of cigarettes a day for the last 25 years. He has pain in the calf with ambulation after 1 block. The leg feels better when he sits with his legs down. He has no numbness. There is no pain at rest. He does not ambulate more than to the mailbox currently because of pain. On exam, he has an antalgic gait with poor hair growth in the right lower limb. He does not have any ulcers. Lumbar exam is normal. Sensation is decreased to light touch on the right lower limb. The right lower limb is mildly erythematous and edematous. There is tenderness to palpation of the right leg. Pulse is not present in the right dorsalis pedis, weak in the popliteal space, and strong in the right femoral artery. Pulses are present in the left lower limb. (Note: Recall the 5P's of critical limb ischemia: Pulses, Pallor, Pain, Paresthesias, and Paralysis)

What workup would you order?

3. Ankle Brachial Index (ABI), CBC, vascular ultrasound, and HgbA1C, ESR/CRP

The patient is diagnosed with critical limb ischemia and undergoes a below the knee amputation (BKA). He follows up with you 1 month post-surgically. What interval history and examination would you like to know?

4. He was fully independent prior to the surgery. The patient states that he was ambulating with some difficulty using crutches. He requires occasional assistance with

ADLs from his family. On exam, his strength and sensation are fully intact in the residual limb. His range of motion is intact. He is alert and oriented x4. He has phantom limb pain. His vision is normal. Surgical incision is well healed without drainage or skin lesions. Edema and pitting are minimal. There is no tenderness. Staples are removed. Passive and active ROM at the knee and hip are full. Sensation is normal. Strength is 5/5 in all extremities including the right residual limb. Labs previously drawn note HgbA1C of 12 and he continues to report limited blood sugar control.

How would you manage this patient post-operatively?

5. Optimize nutrition, anemia, blood sugar and pain control to maximize wound healing. An open incision or wound should be covered with a Telfa® pad under the shrinkage device or prosthesis. Stump shrinker with sock should be worn 24 hours a day.

Temporary prosthesis may be used at 3 to 6 months post surgery (until maximal stump shrinkage has been achieved). The patient should be fitted with a temporary prosthesis to help with shrinking and shaping of the residual limb. Start early prosthetic training (gait and functional training). In a patient whose ambulatory status is uncertain, temporary prosthesis can be used as a trial. Once the residual limb volume has stabilized, a permanent prosthesis is fitted and replaced every 3-5 years.

Other postoperative goals of preprosthetic management include education about prosthetic fitting and care. PT should be initiated for maintaining ROM and strengthening. OT should be initiated for ADL's. Neuropsychology should be consulted for coping. Social

Work should be consulted for community reintegration. Nursing may be needed for diabetic and CHF education and management.

Advanced Concepts in Post-Operative Management:

- Removable rigid dressing (RRD) - Plaster or fiberglass rigid dressing, prevents edema, protects from trauma, and decreases postoperative pain.

- Postoperative dressing - Postoperative edema occurs within a few minutes, so immediate replacement of the dressing is necessary.

- Shrinker socks/elastic bandages - Provide uniform compression: should fit snugly and reach the groin, should also be worn 24-hours a day except for bathing, and may be discontinued after fitting the definitive prosthesis if the amputee wears the prosthesis regularly

- Contracture prevention - No pillow under the back, thigh, or between legs. Also, no head of the bed elevation, and no prolonged sitting. Start crutch walking, and prone lying 15 minutes per day.

- Cleaning - Cleanse daily with soap and warm water and pat dry.

- Scar management - Provide gentle massage along with deep friction massage perpendicular to the scar to prevent scar adhesions. Ensure scar has mobility in all directions.

---

6. The patient is ready for definitive device fitting at 6 months. What device would you fit on this patient?

The prosthetic device would depend on cost, the type of setting a patient lives in (i.e. rural setting – exoskeletal shank), preference for weight of device (exoskeleton heavier, endoskeleton lighter, but has more parts), age of patient, changes in limb size with time (atrophy), the patient's occupation, and lifestyle. Also, suspension (cuff, brim, sleeve, silicone suction pin), shank, and prosthetic foot (SACH, flex, multi-axis).

Advanced Concepts for Prosthetics:

- AKA Components: Socket (Ischial containment – narrow mediolateral, higher trim line, stabilizes the relationship between the pelvis and proximal femur vs. Quadrilateral, and wide mediolateral ischial tuberosity sits on brim), Suspension (suction, belt), Knee unit (manual locking, single axis, stance control, polycentric, fluid controlled), and Prosthetic foot

- Patellar tendon bearing (PTB) socket - standard socket used for BKA

- Silicone liners - without the suspension pin, helps manage shear problems that can occur with split thickness skin grafts.

- Solid ankle cushioned-heel (SACH) foot - common prosthetic foot that is durable, lightweight, has compressible heel and wooden keel allowing it to simulate the motions of the ankle in normal walking without actual ankle movement occurring.

- Multi-axis foot - athletic activities or uneven terrain

- Flex foot - energy storing foot

- Energy expenditure increase - unilateral BKA 25%, bilateral BKA 50%, unilateral AKA 100%, bilateral AKA 250%

7. The patient returns 1 year later and insists he wants a set of "blade runners". He is ambulatory in the household setting and does not walk long distances. How do you respond?

Mr. Smith, I can see you are very hopeful. Can you tell me a little bit more to help me understand what you are feeling? ("I'm motivated to get fit. I'm sick of my health problems and not being able to move. I'm too young for this.") Mr. Smith, I can respect what you're feeling. I'm happy to see that you're motivated to get healthier. ("Yes, I'm motivated. I want to get better, and with blade runners I think I can be more active.") I am committed to working with you and getting you to where you want to be. Let's move one step at a time as a team. I'll call your insurance company to see if we can change you to a multi-axis foot, get you into PT, and see if we can walk longer distance. Let's set up another appointment in a few months to touch base and if you're walking well and at longer distances, let's see if we can advance you to those energy storing feet. ("Yes, that would be nice. Thank you so much, doctor.")

Advanced Concepts for Activity Level:

- K0 - non-ambulatory; not eligible for prosthetic device
- K1 - household ambulator - SACH foot, single-axis knee
- K2 - community ambulator - multi-axis foot, single axis knee
- K3 - engages in exercise activity, ambulation with variable cadence -energy storing foot, pneumatic/fluid knee
- K4 - high impact activity/ athlete - any ankle or knee system

References:

Gabriel, V., Holavanahalli, R., & Braddom, R. (2011). Physical Medicine & Rehabilitation. Philadelphia: Elsevier Saunders.

Meier RH 3rd, Melton D. (2014). Ideal functional outcomes for amputation levels. Phys Med Rehabil Clin N Am.Feb;25(1):199-212. doi: 10.1016/j.pmr.2013.09.011. Review. PubMed PMID: 24287248.

Klarich J, Brueckner I. (2014). Amputee rehabilitation and preprosthetic care. Phys Med Rehabil Clin N Am. Feb;25(1):75-91. doi: 10.1016/j.pmr.2013.09.005. Review. PubMed PMID: 24287241.

Case: MSK Disorders

1. A 45-years-old male with right knee pain worse in the morning presents to your clinic. What history and physical examination findings would you like to know?

2. The patient has a history of hypertension. He has pain in the knee with swelling for the last month. Previously he had right ankle pain with swelling, followed by wrist pain with swelling. He reports no recent illness or travel. He has no numbness or weakness. He denies any rashes. He has morning stiffness. He denies fevers, chills, diarrhea, or blurry vision. Upon exam, his knee appears normal. Hip exam is normal. Sensation and strength are normal. There is mild tenderness along the patellar tendon. Reflexes are normal. Ankle exam is normal. Lung and heart sounds are normal.

What workup would you order?

3. CBC, CMP, HgbA1C, ESR/CRP, UA, RF, CK, HLAB27, Iron, Ferritin, haptoglobin, fibrinogen, Calcium, Joint Aspiration and culture and microscopy (if effusion present), and x-ray.

Inflammatory diseases will cause abnormalities in many routine laboratory studies. There may be anemia, and elevated or decreased platelet count and/or white blood cell count. Leukopenia and thrombocytopenia are common in patients with SLE. If there is a joint effusion, aspiration and fluid studies may be indicated. Auto antibody labs may be helpful.

Advanced Concepts in Laboratory exam:

- Gout - Uric acid does not show up on x-rays, monosodium urate crystals negatively birefringent

- CPPD - Calcium in pseudogout can be seen on an x-ray, positively birefringent

- Rheumatoid Factor - sensitivity 70%, specificity 70%, 20% RA patients are seronegative, positive in 15% of normal adults

- Anti-Cyclic Citrullinated Peptide: sensitivity 70%, specificity 95% for RA, JIA, psoriatic arthritis, Lupus, Sjögren's syndrome, inflammatory myopathies and active tuberculosis

- Anti-Sm: Sensitivity 15%, Specificity 99% SLE

- Anti-dsDNA: Sensitivity 70%, Specificity 95% SLE, moderately elevated in most autoimmune conditions

- Antinuclear antibody: Rim, homogenous, speckled, nucleolar; positive in many autoimmune conditions, positive in 50% of normal adults, used when pre-test probability is high for SLE

- Anti-U1RNP: SLE plus systemic sclerosis, mixed connective tissue disease

- Anti-SSA (Ro) / SSB (La): Sjögren's syndrome, some subsets of SLE patients

- Anti-SRP, anti-JO-1, anti-Mi-2 and anti-PM/Scl: autoimmune inflammatory myopathies, scleroderma

- anti-PL12, anti-EJ, anti-OJ, anti-PL7, and anti-KS: more common in PM than DM, rare in children, present with muscle weakness, interstitial lung disease, arthritis and

> fevers
>
> - cANCA: Wegener's Granulomatosis, microscopic polyangiitis, and Churg-Strauss syndrome.
>
> - pANCA: microscopic polyangiitis, vasculitis, inflammatory bowel disease, SLE, RA, and juvenile idiopathic arthritis
>
> - cANCA plus PR3: Wegener's Granulomatosis
>
> - pANCA plus MPO: microscopic polyangiitis, vasculitis
>
> - Low C3/C4: immune complex glomerulonephritis in SLE
>
> - Increased IgA: Inflammatory bowel disease

What is your differential diagnosis?

4. Rheumatologic condition should be considered particularly with polyarticular inflammatory arthritis that is accompanied by tendinopathy and morning stiffness. Other differentials include infection, cancer, and overuse injuries.

> **Advanced Concepts in Differential Diagnosis:**
>
> - Inflammatory: AM stiffness >1hr, swelling, symptoms improve with activity, systemic symptoms, and fatigue
>
> - Non-inflammatory: AM stiffness <30 min, symptoms better with rest, lack of systemic symptoms
>
> - SLE: 95% ANA positive, malar rash
>
> - Mixed connective tissue disorder

- Cryoglobulinemia
- Scleroderma
- Polymyositis/dermatomyositis: heliotrope rash
- Rheumatoid arthritis: chronic, symmetric erosive synovitis develops in the joints and leads to articular destruction
- Sjogren's Syndrome: dry eyes and mucous membranes
- Hashimoto's thyroiditis
- Vasculitis - reticular rash, Henoch-Schonlein purpura (Palpable purpura)
- Reactive arthritis: balanitis, conjunctivitis, uveitis
- Polymyalgia Rheumatica: prednisone
- Ankylosing Spondylitis: AM stiffness >30 min, Improvement with exercise, awaking with back pain 2nd half of night, alternating buttock pain (2/4 sensitivity 70%, specificity 80%)
- Psoriasis
- Inflammatory bowel disease
- Temporal Artery: biopsy, prednisone
- Grave's disease
- Autoimmune hepatitis: elevations of transaminases, bilirubin, and serum proteins
- Sarcoidosis: Hypercalcemia can be observed in approximately 30% of patients with sarcoidosis
- Primary Biliary Cirrhosis

- Discoid Lupus
- Celiac disease
- Autoimmune hemolytic anemia
- Viral: Hepatitis C, endocarditis, TB, HIV
- Raynaud's: scleroderma, SLE, DM/PM, MCTD
- Oral ulcers: SLE, Behcets
- Enthesopathy: Reiter's, ankylosing spondylitis, psoriasis, and inflammatory bowel disease
- Nodules: RA, gout
- Hemochromatosis: hepatic cirrhosis, cardiomyopathy, diabetes mellitus, and pituitary dysfunction

The patient is diagnosed with reactive arthritis. How would you manage this patient?

5. The patient should be referred to Rheumatology. Ophthalmology should be consulted to monitor eyes. PT should be initiated for maintaining ROM. Therapy may progress to isometrics once inflammation is controlled. Strengthening program should be engaged with caution. OT may be initiated for any upper limb involvement or contractures. Neuropsychology should be consulted for coping. Social Work should be consulted for community reintegration or in-home support if there is need. Nursing may be needed for medication education particularly if there is need for subcutaneous injections. Pain control may include NSAIDS and acetaminophen.

6. The patient returns 4 months later and insists he wants to run a marathon. What do you say?

Mr. Smith, I can see you are very hopeful. Can you tell me a little bit more to help me understand what you are feeling? ("I'm motivated to get healthy. I will not let my medical problem define me. I'm too young for this.") Mr. Smith, I can respect what you're feeling. I'm happy to see that you're motivated to take control of your life. ("Yes, I'm motivated.") I am committed to working with you and getting you to where you want to be. Let's move one step at a time as a team. Let's progress with your physical therapist and see if we can start you on shorter distance running. We can set up another appointment in a few weeks to touch base and run labs and see how your body responds to the stress. ("Yes, that would be nice. Thank you so much, doctor.")

References:

American College of Rheumatology Clinical Guidelines. https://www.rheumatology.org/Practice-Quality/Clinical-Support/Clinical-Practice-Guidelines

Birtane M, Yavuz S, Tastekin N. (2017). Laboratory evaluation of rheumatic diseases. World J Methodol. 2017 Mar 26; 7(1): 1–8. doi: 10.5662/wjm.v7.i1.1

Cuccurullo MD, Dr. Sara J.. Physical Medicine and Rehabilitation Board Review, Third Edition. Springer Publishing Company. Kindle Edition.

Case: MSK Disorders

1. A 25-years-old female presents to your clinic with right ankle pain that worsens after dancing. What history and physical examination would you like to know?

2. The patient has no significant medical history. She has had pain in the ankle without swelling for the last month. Previously, she had intermittent pain in the ankle and left ankle sprain remotely. She reports no recent illness or travel. She has no numbness or weakness. She denies any rashes, fevers, chills, diarrhea, or blurry vision. Upon exam, her ankle appears normal. Knee exam is normal. Sensation and strength are normal. There is mild tenderness along the lateral malleolus. Reflexes are normal. Lung and heart sounds are normal.

What workup would you order?

3. X-ray, MRI, EMG/NCS; consider CBC, CMP, HgbA1C, ESR/CRP, UA, RF, CK, HLAB27, Joint Aspiration with culture and microscopy.

Ankle pain in a young female has a few differentials. Be sure to include rheumatologic differentials as well as common MSK differentials.

> **Advanced Concepts in Imaging:**
>
> MRI Findings of Posterior Ankle Impingement:
>
> - T1: low signal in areas of bone bruising
> - T2/STIR: high signal posterior to ankle in areas of bone bruising
> - PD/PD fat saturated: high signal posterior to the ankle

X-ray:

- Lateral view is important for exostoses on distal anterior and dorsal talar neck including Stieda process or os trigonum.

- Oblique anteromedial view has a higher sensitivity for detecting tibial and talar osteophytes.

- Os trigonum is best viewed with lateral view with ankle in a 25 degrees external rotation.

What is your differential diagnosis?

Advanced Concepts in Differential Diagnosis:

- Os Trigonum: one of the bony ossicles of the foot posterior to the talus on the lateral foot radiograph - represents a failure of fusion of the lateral tubercle of the posterior process in 10% of adults, most common cause of posterior impingement

- Stieda process: elongated lateral tubercle of the posterior process of the talus considered an anatomical variant formed from a secondary ossification center at the posterolateral aspect of the talus

- Subtalar/tibiotalar joint degeneration: may have associated osteophyte, hypertrophic capsule and synovium

- Achilles Tendinopathy: Pain is usually more shallow than posterior impingement.

- Plantar fasciitis: often associated with tight heel cord

- ATFL sprain: common with inversion injuries

- Deltoid sprain: Posterior deltoid fibers may become

> inflamed or scarred from repetitive impingement.
>
> - Posteromedial Impingement: posteromedial tibiotalar capsule and posterior fibers of the tibiotalar ligament impingement between talus and medial malleolus during supination
>
> - Posterolateral impingement: posterior talofibular ligament anatomic variant present in 60% of the population, entrapment during plantar flexion
>
> - Talar or calcaneal fractures
>
> - Flexor hallucis longus entrapment: entrapment from running between medial and lateral posterior process of talus, may have variant of intermalleolar ligament
>
> - Retrocalcaneal bursitis
>
> - Posterior tibial osteochondral injuries
>
> - Tarsal tunnel syndrome
>
> - Tibiofibular ligament/capsular inflammation, scarring, and thickening

The patient is diagnosed with posterior ankle impingement from repetitive plantar flexion stress with associated synovial hypertrophy and bony edema. What is your treatment plan?

5. Start with relative rest followed by PT. Pain control may include NSAIDS and acetaminophen. If the patient is refractory to treatment, arthroscopic surgical resection may be pursued.

The patient returns 6 months post surgical resection with continued pain and continues to dance on her injury. She is worried that she will lose her position with a prestigious dance company. What do you say?

6. Ms. Smith, I can see you are very distressed. Can you tell me a little bit more to help me understand what you are feeling? ("I need to dance. If I don't perform, they will replace me.") Ms. Smith, I can respect what you're feeling. This is a difficult situation. ("Yes, I trained my whole life for this. I can't lose it.") I am committed to working with you and getting you to where you want to be. Let's move one step at a time as a team. Let's get you back into physical therapy to see if we can get you through this season. During the off season, let's take a break from pointe shoe dancing and aggressively modify how you load the ankle and work with the physical therapist. We can set up another appointment in a few weeks to touch base and monitor that ankle while you dance to make sure it's not getting worse with the dancing. ("Yes, that would be nice. Thank you so much, doctor.")

References:

Cuccurullo MD, Dr. Sara J.. Physical Medicine and Rehabilitation Board Review, Third Edition. Springer Publishing Company. Kindle Edition.

Lavery et. al. (2016). Ankle Impingement. *J Orthop Surg Res*. Sept. 11(1):97

Russell JA, et al. (2010). Pathoanatomy of posterior ankle impingement in ballet dancers. *Clin Anat*. 23(6):613-21

Case: Neuromuscular

1. A 9-years-old male with his mother presents to your office with a 4 weeks history of worsening weakness. What history and physical examination findings would you like to know?

2. The patient has a 4 weeks history with progressive weakness. There is no numbness. There is no shortness of breath or palpitations. He was able to ambulate until 4 weeks ago. He has mental retardation and was previously diagnosed with "cerebral palsy". He has trouble getting out of a chair and started using a wheelchair. He has abnormal facies on exam. He is thin and hypotonic and has 2 / 5 strength in the pelvic girdle and 1 / 5 in the distal lower limbs. His sensation is intact. Reflexes are 0 in the upper and lower limbs. Cranial nerves are intact. Heart sounds and lung sounds are normal. There is no family history of similar disorder. Patient reached all milestones, but they were all severely delayed. The patient has never had any treatment or work up. The family denies any recent illnesses. (Important factors to consider include age of onset, developmental milestones, familial involvement, and prodromal illness. On exam, look for atrophy, hypertrophy, abnormal MSR, weakness, hypotonia, gait abnormalities, or myotonia.)

What kind of work up do you initiate?

3. Work up should include genetic testing, muscle biopsy, CK, aldolase, CMP, CBC, ESR/CRP, brain MRI, lumbar MRI, and EMG/NCS. Genetic testing has demonstrated a greater ability to classify the type of myopathy.

What is your differential diagnosis for this patient?

4. The most likely diagnosis is: myopathic disorder, mitochondrial disorder, congenital myopathies, inflammatory myopathies, or spina bifida.

Advanced Concepts for Differential Diagnosis:

- Duchenne Muscular dystrophy – proximal weakness, 5 years-old onset, no dystrophin, increased CPK, EKG abnormal, oculomotor spared, mental retardation, delay in walking, pseudohypertrophy, proximal muscle weakness, legs > arms, frequent falls, creatinine kinase grossly elevated, EMG myopathic, and ultrasound increased hypoechogenicity in muscles

- Becker's – proximal weakness, cardiomyopathy, decreased dystrophin, increased CPK, later onset, pseudohypertrophy, proximal muscle weakness, legs > arms, and frequent falls.

- Hereditary Motor Sensory Neuropathy (HMSN) - Stork (or champagne bottle) leg appearance, focal atrophy of distal lower extremity muscles

- Glycogen storage disease/metabolic myopathy - Hepatosplenomegaly, acid maltase deficiency, and Types 3 and 4 glycogenosis.

- Myotonic Dystrophy – more distal myotonia, EKG abnormal, type I fiber atrophy, type II fiber hypertrophy, Dilantin, procainamide, and calcium channel blockers; Hatchet face / Craniofacial changes, and dental malocclusion (Note: Myotonia is a painless delayed relaxation of skeletal muscles following a voluntary contraction, exacerbated by cold but relieved with exercise.)

- Arthrogryposis - fixed deformity of the extremities due to intrauterine hypomobility, may occur in newborns from myopathies, muscular dystrophies, or oligohydramnios. A hallmark sign of myopathy is the inability to generate a forceful contraction.

- Facioscapulohumeral dystrophy – proximal muscle weakness, facial droop, Popeye arm (forearm and deltoid sparing arm atrophy), EMG tibialis anterior and deltoid, scattered fiber necrosis and regeneration

- Central core – delayed milestones, proximal weakness, malignant hyperthermia, Type I fiber central core, and absent mitochondria

- Nemaline rod myopathy- diffuse weakness, face abnormalities, and rod-shaped bodies on Gomori trichrome stain

- Centronuclear myotubular – hypotonia, dysphagia, and central location of fiber nuclei

- Fiber type disproportion – hypotonia, hip contracture and dislocation, and small Type 1 and large Type II fibers

- Polymyositis – proximal symmetric weakness, periorbital rash, Gottron's sign, Type I and II necrosis, EMG AA in paraspinals, and older patient

- Inclusion body myositis – asymmetric proximal and distal weakness, rimmed cytoplasmic vacuoles, eosinophilic inclusion bodies, NCS abnormal SNAP, and older patient

- SMA I – never sit, hyper/atrophic fibers, hypotonia, and CK normal

- SMA II- independent sitting, hypotonia, CK normal

- SMA III – symmetric weakness legs more than arms, CK nml, higher educational level, physically need help, at the spinal cord level, prognosis, and muscle fasciculations common

- Milestones: 6 month to sit, 2 word phrases at 2yo

- Myopathic gait- hyperlordotic, waddling gait caused by weakness of back and hip extensors which produces anterior pelvic tilt and a tendency for the trunk to be positioned anteriorly to the hip (lumbar hyperlordosis) which positions their center of gravity posterior to the hip and stabilizes the hip in extension

- Spina Bifida - greater than 90% with myelomeningocele will have neurogenic bladder

5. The patient is diagnosed with Becker's Muscular Dystrophy. What is your comprehensive rehabilitation plan for this patient?

Referral to Pulmonary services is required for FVC monitoring. If contractures are present, consider referral to Orthopedics for surgical opinion regarding tendon lengthening. Referral to Cardiology may be needed for EKG and monitoring for arrhythmias. If seizures are present, the patient will need referral to Neurology for anti-epileptic medications and EEG. The patient will need PT for isometric exercises, custom wheelchair fitting, possible bracing for scoliosis, and bracing to avoid contractures. Neuropsychology may be consulted to counsel patient and family on life expectancy and loss of function. Social work can help with community integration particularly school, transportation, and community resources.

> **Advanced Concepts for Management:**
>
> - Scoliosis - Bracing is not helpful to correct neuromuscular condition related scoliosis, but can be used for positioning in wheelchair. Wheelchair fitting is important to prevent skin breakdown since incidence is high for neuromuscular disorders (approximately 80-90%). For FVC >35% & curves >20%, consider surgery for correction of scoliosis.
>
> - Spina bifida - Independent self-catheterization may be achieved at the age of 5 to 6 years. 15% to 20% have vesicoureteral reflux at birth. Scoliosis occurs secondary to loss of truncal support and is seen in 70% of patients above L2 and 40% below L4. Caution regarding latex allergy.
>
> - Myotonia – Keep limbs warm, and Dilantin
>
> - Polymyositis – Steroids

6. The patient and family follows up with you and want to take the patient to Mexico for stem cell treatment. They want your opinion. How do you respond?

Mrs. Smith, I can see you are very hopeful. Can you tell me a little bit more to help me understand what you are feeling? ("I'm really hopeful. They are charging me $30,000 for treating Jimmy and state there will be 50% improvement.") Mrs. Smith, I can respect what you're feeling. Stem cells are promising, but I want to caution you about the cost and over promise. There isn't much research to support these claims. ("There isn't? I'm not sure what to do. We have to do something!") I am committed to working with you and doing the best we can for Jimmy. Let's look at all the possibilities. Let's call the clinic together and see if they can give us more information. Let's set up another appointment in a few days to touch base and set up a time to call them. ("Yes, that would be nice. Thank you so much, doctor.")

References:

American Association of Orthopedic Surgery. https://orthoinfo.aaos.org/en/diseases-conditions/neuromuscular-scoliosis/

Allam AM, Schwabe AL. (2013). Neuromuscular scoliosis. *PMR*. Nov;5(11):957-63. doi: 10.1016/j.pmrj.2013.05.015. Review. PubMed PMID: 24247014.

Kang PB et al. (2015). Guideline Development Subcommittee of the American Academy of Neurology and the Practice Issues Review Panel of the American Association of Neuromuscular & Electrodiagnostic Medicine. Evidence-based guideline summary: evaluation, diagnosis, and management of congenital muscular dystrophy: Report of the Guideline Development Subcommittee of the American Academy of Neurology and the Practice Issues Review Panel of the American Association of Neuromuscular & Electrodiagnostic Medicine. Neurology. Mar 31;84(13):1369-78. doi: 10.1212/WNL.0000000000001416. PubMed PMID: 25825463; PubMed Central PMCID: PMC4388744.

Case: SCI

1. A 30-years-old male presents to your office for management of T4 ASIA A after a car accident 1 month ago. What would you like to know regarding this patient's history and physical examination?

2. This patient was in a rollover car accident 1 month ago. There was no loss of consciousness. He was admitted to an inpatient unit for 3 weeks and discharged home a few days ago. He underwent a spinal fusion at T4 for a burst fracture. He has no control of bowel or bladder. He has been using a catheter. His primary concern is episodes of urinary incontinence between catheterizations every 4-6 hours, worsening. He has no other medical problems. He takes some pain medications provided on discharge from rehabilitation. He denies fever or chills or worsening spasticity. He has an elevated temperature on vital signs, is alert and follows all commands. He has no sensation below T4. He is hyperreflexic in the lower limbs. He has clear lungs and normal heart sounds.

What is your work up for this patient?

3. A urine analysis should be ordered along with CBC, BMP, and ESR. A bladder scan should be ordered to look for urine volume.

What is your differential diagnosis for the etiology of his worsening urinary incontinence?

4. The most common cause of urinary incontinence after SCI is return of micturition reflex, urinary tract infection, and overflow incontinence.

> **Advanced Concepts for Differential Diagnosis:**
>
> - TBI - TBI should be considered for higher level SCI or for high velocity accidents. It may lead to poor cognition with poor awareness of need to void. Timed voiding should be used to manage TBI associated incontinence.
>
> - Stroke / dissection - Strokes may be considered for higher level SCI, particularly if they lead to vascular compromise in older individuals. CT scan is the imaging modality of choice for acute strokes.
>
> - BPH - BPH related flow issues should also be a differential in older male patients.
>
> - Syringomyelia - This should be a consideration for SCI injuries that are more remote. MRI of the cervical spine should be conducted.

5. The UA is positive for a urinary tract infection.

What is your management plan?

6. Physician concerns include starting oral antibiotics for 7 days for hospital/catheter associated infection. The physician should follow up on the culture to ensure that the oral antibiotics are sensitive. The patient will need to monitor bladder volume and voiding schedule. The patient may be having overflow incontinence particularly if oral intake volumes are too high. Additionally, comprehensive rehabilitation should be initiated with PT for strengthening, mobility needs, and additional equipment needs. Occupational therapy should be initiated for ADL's, driving, and dressing. Speech therapy should be prescribed for any cognition issues. Neuropsychology should be consulted for any emotional and psychological issues

related to accident and new SCI status. Social work may help with reintegration back into the community and work.

7. The patient's worsened incontinence resolved with a 1 week course of oral antibiotics. However, the patient follows up with you in 8 weeks with recurrent incontinence issues for 3 days. Work up is negative including bladder scan showing volumes <100cc. You believe that the patient is having return of the micturition reflex. How do you counsel the patient?

8. Mr. Smith, I believe that your bladder control may be returning. I am very hopeful. What do you think? ("I'm very embarrassed. I'd rather use a catheter. Now, I lose my bladder when I'm out and have to wear a diaper. It's embarrassing.") Mr. Smith, I can respect what you're feeling. This is an extremely difficult situation. ("Yes, it is. I don't want to smell or have to change in public-I'm terrified to even go outside!") I am committed to working with you and getting you to the most functional state as possible. Let's switch some of your medication. Let's get you on an improved time voiding schedule. The incontinence should improve in the next couple weeks or so, and there may be return of bladder function. Let's get you set up with Urology. Let's set up another appointment in a few days to touch base. ("Oh good, that sounds more hopeful. Yes, that would be nice. Thank you so much, doctor.")

References:

Tai et al. Spinal reflex control of micturition after spinal cord injury. *Restor Neurol Neurosci*. 2006; 24(2): 69–78.

Carter GT. (2014). Spinal cord injury rehabilitation. *Phys Med Rehabil Clin N Am*. Aug;25(3):xiii-xiv. doi: 10.1016/j.pmr.2014.07.001. PubMed PMID: 25064796.

Case: TBI

1. An 18-years-old male presents to your office with 4 weeks history of headache after a head injury during a soccer game.

What history and physical examination would you like to know?

2. The pain has been present for 4 weeks. He has been staying in a dark room and hasn't been able to go to school. He did not lose consciousness during the soccer game and was able to play the rest of the game without issues, and was also not seen by a physician until today. He has nausea and blurry vision. He denies any memory issues. He has trouble falling asleep. He denies dizziness or balance issues. He admits to irritability. On examination his strength and sensation are fully intact. Reflexes are normal. Pupils are equal and reactive to light. He is alert and oriented to place, time, and situation. Cranial nerves are intact. GCS is 15.

What is your differential diagnosis for this patient?

3. The most likely differentials are sports related concussion/mild TBI, moderate or severe TBI, migraine headache, epidural hematoma, subdural hematoma, or AVM. Other differential diagnosis are spinal cord injury, fracture, tumor, dehydration, or depression.

Advanced Concepts for Differential Diagnosis:

- Second impact syndrome - A second brain injury during the post concussive phase that causes rapid decompensation into semi-comatose state likely secondary to impairment in the brain's vascular autoregulation, leading to engorgement and increased ICP that results in herniation.

- Post concussive syndrome - per the Berlin consensus, the persistence of concussion symptoms beyond the normal course of recovery (2-4 weeks), usually lasting 3-6 months after TBI

- Moderate TBI - loss of consciousness, amnesia less than 24 hours, and initial GCS 9-12.

- Sports related concussion - Symptoms (headache, feeling like in a fog, lability), Physical signs (possibly loss of consciousness, amnesia, neurological deficit), Balance impairment (gait unsteadiness), Behavioral changes (irritability), Cognitive impairment (slowed reaction times), Sleep/wake disturbance (somnolence, drowsiness)

What kind of work up do you initiate?

5. Head x-ray, followed by head CT scan, or brain MRI are all appropriate imaging modalities to be considered. However, there is limited utility of these modalities unless there is decreasing level of consciousness, increasing severity of signs and symptoms, persistent focal neurologic deficit, etc., to assess associated injuries including intracranial bleed, cerebral edema, diffuse axonal injury, and/or skull fracture. Use cervical imaging as well when cervical spine injury is suspected.

> **Advanced Concepts for Work Up:**
>
> - Biomarkers (S-100 proteins, neuron specific enolase, tau protein) - inconclusive for identifying individuals with concussion and represents research that may one day be clinically applicable, although Brain Trauma Indicator lab test (UCH-L1 and GFAP) was recently approved by the FDA for evaluation of mild TBI
>
> - Event- and evoke-related potentials - Inconclusive for the clinical management of concussion at this time and represents research that may one day be clinically applicable.
>
> - Brief neuropsychological (NP) test (SCAT5) - assessment of attention and memory function

6. MRI is normal. Based on SCAT5 testing, you diagnose the patient with post-concussion syndrome.

What is your rehabilitation plan for this patient?

> **Advanced Concepts for Treatment:**
>
> - Return to play guide - Rest initially with cessation of sport, then stepwise return to play advanced as tolerated and once asymptomatic during the preceding stage. Step 1: Light aerobic activity to increase heart rate for 5 to 10 minutes. Step 2: Moderate intensity activity with limited body and head movement. Step 3: Heavy, non-contact activity including drills. Step 4: Practice and full contact. Step 5: Return to competition.
> - Return to play should be individualized

7. The physician should be actively considering medication for sleep and sleep hygiene education. A referral to concussion specialist may be considered.

Neuropsychological testing may be initiated. PT should be prescribed for any balance issues. OT may be prescribed for any fine motor deficits. Speech may be prescribed for memory or cognitive issues. A graduated return to play should be initiated with the consultation of a concussion specialist. There should be close communication with the team coach and Athletic Trainer if patient/family provides permission (Remember HIPAA). The patient and family need to be counseled regarding return to play. Cognitive rest beyond the initial 24 hours is controversial.

8. The patient follows up with you in 4 weeks and continues to have symptoms and is extremely upset. He states he needs to be back in the game or he will lose his chance at a career in soccer. How do you respond?

9. Mr. Smith, I can see you are very distressed. Can you tell me a little bit more to help me understand what you are feeling? ("I'm worried about my position. If I don't go back, I'll lose my shot at scholarships and a professional career and my entire future as an athlete.") Mr. Smith, I can respect what you're feeling. This is an extremely difficult situation. ("Yes, it is. This is my future. Soccer is all I know.") I am committed to working with you and getting you back into the game, and helping you with your future career as an athlete. Let's evaluate adjusting your medications. I'll also call your coach with you and ask your parents' permission to see what we can have you doing for the time being. I'll also call your Concussion Specialist to see if there's anything additional we can do. Let's set up another appointment in a few days to touch base. ("Yes, that would be nice. Thank you so much, doctor.")

References:

PubMed Health. (2018). Post-concussion Syndrome. PubMed. https://www.ncbi.nlm.nih.gov/pubmedhealth/PMHT0024860

Bay, Ostik. (2009). Second Impact Syndrome. West J Emerg Med. 2009 Feb; 10(1): 6–10.

Center for Disease Control and Prevention. https://www.cdc.gov/headsup/providers/return_to_activities.html

AAOS Concussion (Mild Traumatic Brain Injury) and the Team Physician: A Consensus Statement—2011 Update. https://www.sportsmed.org/AOSSMIMIS/members/downloads/education/ConsensusStatements/Concussion.pdf

McRoy et al. (2016). Consensus statement on concussion in sport—the 5th international conference on concussion in sport held in Berlin.

Case: Neurorehabilitation

The director of rehabilitation at a local skilled nursing facility (SNF) places a consult for you to see an 89-year-old female who has failed to process in SNF-based physical therapy program due to poor lower extremity function.

1. What history would you like to know?

She is a long-term resident of the SNF, with a medical history of prior stroke 3 years ago with residual right-sided hemiparesis. She had a diagnosis of dementia and can follow simple one step commands. She was re-enrolled into the SNF based physical therapy program after discharge from acute admission for sepsis due to UTI two weeks ago for deconditioning and ADL dysfunction related to acute inpatient stay. Prior level of function was minimum assist for transfers and gait with front wheel walker. Current level of function is moderate assist for transfers and maximum assist for 5 steps with front wheel walker. The physical therapist reports that the patient has had difficulty with hip extension and knee extension. There is reported increased spasticity according to the treating therapist. Previously, she was on baclofen which upon review has fallen off of her medication list.

2. What physical examination would you do?

No new skin lesions on exam. She can follow one step commands. She denies pain to palpation of the right upper and lower extremities. She has impaired sensation to light touch in both right upper and lower extremities. She has increased tone in her right upper and lower extremities,

Modified Ashworth Scale 2. She has full passive range of motion to her right shoulder, minus 5 degrees of right elbow extension, and minus 5 degrees of right wrist extension. She has minus 15 degrees of right hip extension and 15 of right knee extension. Her strength is 3- /5 grossly in her right upper and lower right extremity.

3. Based on the history and physical exam findings, what is your differential diagnosis?

Increased spasticity due to withdrawal of medication, Superimposed deconditioning on residual right hemiparesis from stroke, New stroke with worsening impairment, Joint contracture, Infection, and Lower extremity fracture.

4. What diagnostics would you order for this patient?

Urinary analysis, CBC, and CMP, to rule out infection and metabolic causes of increased spasticity. XR right hip, right knee, right elbow, right wrist, consideration for fracture, heterotrophic ossification. Consider repeat brain imaging if suspicious of a new stroke or other intracranial process.

5. Assuming the diagnosis is increased spasticity due to withdrawal of baclofen what is your plan for management?

Stepwise re-initiation of baclofen. Monitor progress of medication with follow up visits with up titration, as necessary. Work with physical therapy regarding the need for stretching and range of motion to minimize further risk of contracture. Physical modalities such as ice/heat, TENS can be considered to reduce spasticity temporarily prior to hands on therapy. Consider splinting to prevent further contracture. Consideration for chemodenervation injections in refractory cases with clear goals, such as hygiene considerations, ADL considerations, and splinting considerations.

6. The medical director of the skilled nursing facility has asked you to help reduce medication errors from rehabilitation readmissions. How would you go about this?

Identify key stakeholders including management, nursing, and pharmacies that may help identify causes for medical errors. Implement a root cause analysis and consider using a standard process such as PDCA: Plan-Do-Check-Act. Discuss with medical directors, head of nursing, and pharmacy directors for avenues of intervention/plans.

7. Roleplaying the situation: The patient's son is at bedside with questions about obtaining a functional electrical stimulation orthosis for his mother to help her with feeding herself. His friend's father has a similar device after his stroke and is doing well with it. He is wondering if you would be able to write a prescription for the device.

Be empathetic and acknowledge the concern for his mother and her function. Express that it is difficult to compare his mother's situation to his friend's father's situation. However, considering her current function including spasticity, contracture and diagnosis of dementia it is unlikely that she would benefit considerably with the device. Offer alternatives.

References:

O'dwyer, N. J., Ada, L., & Neilson, P. D. (1996). Spasticity and muscle contracture following stroke. Brain, 119(5), 1737-1749.

Patrick, E., & Ada, L. (2006). The Tardieu Scale differentiates contracture from spasticity whereas the Ashworth Scale is confounded by it. Clinical rehabilitation, 20(2), 173-182.

Johnson, C. N. (2002). The benefits of PDCA. Quality Progress, 35(5), 120.

Peters, H. T., Page, S. J., & Persch, A. (2017). Giving them a hand: wearing a myoelectric elbow-wrist-hand orthosis reduces upper extremity impairment in chronic stroke. Archives of physical medicine and rehabilitation, 98(9), 1821-1827.wrist-hand orthosis reduces upper extremity impairment in chronic stroke. Archives of physical medicine and rehabilitation. 2017 Sep 1;98(9):1821-7.

Case: Wrist Drop

A 29-year-old otherwise healthy male with history of a nondisplaced left mid-shaft humerus fracture treated non-surgically is referred to your office from orthopedics for left wrist drop.

1. What would you like to know about his history and physical examination?

He was involved in a snowboarding accident and fell onto his left side. He was splinted and then casted for 6-weeks and had close follow up with orthopedics. He just had his cast removed. Soon after the accident, he was unable to extend the wrist and the fingers; elbow flexion, supination, and grip were also weak. He has noticed gradual improvement straightening his elbow and extending his wrist. He is now able to hold his wrist straight for a few minutes before fatiguing. He also has numbness on the back of the hand and forearm that is about "50% less" than normal. He does not have radiating neck pain. Recent x-rays show complete bone healing. On physical examination you find mild weakness of elbow flexion (brachioradialis) and supination with more motor impairment involving wrist and finger extension as well as grip, 4/5. Triceps is normal. Sensation is diminished on the dorsum of the hand and posterior forearm. Reflexes are slightly diminished at left triceps, otherwise intact. Cervical and shoulder examinations are normal.

2. What is the differential diagnosis and what additional tests would you order?

Traumatic or compressive radial mononeuropathy, cervical radiculopathy, and brachial plexopathy. Less likely, other types of radial nerve syndromes (see table), disuse syndrome, or concomitant musculoskeletal injury by nature of trauma.

RADIAL NEUROPATHY CAUSES	
Trauma	External Compression
Mid shaft humeral fractures (most common) Laceration High velocity stretch injury	Proximal arm Use of axillary crutches *Saturday night palsy* or *honeymoon palsy* Spiral groove syndrome Distal (Superficial radial sensory) *Handcuff palsy*
Entrapment	Other
Lateral intermuscular septum of the arm - *Radial tunnel syndrome* Arcade of Frohse at the supinator muscle – *supinator syndrome*	Lead intoxication Mononeuritis multiplex Autoimmune conditions Multifocal Motor Neuropathy (MMN) Tumor

An electrodiagnostic study would be prudent. Your patient returns 1-week later with the report.

Nerve conduction studies:

Sensory	Right	Latency (ms)	Amplitude (mV)	Left	Latency (ms)	Amplitude (microV)	
Median (s)		3.0	57		3.1	60	
Ulnar (s)		2.5	35		2.4	37	
Radial (s)		2.0	28		**4.0**	**5**	
Motor							
	Right	Latency (ms)	Amplitude (mV)	Left	Latency (ms)	Amplitude (mV)	CV (m/s) bilateral
Median (APB) (m) wrist		3.5	11		3.4	12	
Antecubital fossa			11			12	56
Ulnar (ADM) (m) wrist		2.8	14		2.7	14	
Below elbow			14			14	54
Above elbow			13.9			14	53
Radial (EDC) (m) wrist		3.2	8		**5.3**	**6**	
Below spiral groove			7.9			**5.8**	n/a

Above spiral groove			7.9			2	n/a

APB: ABductor pollicis brevis; ADM: ABductor digiti minimi; EDC: extensor digitorum communis; ms: milliseconds, mV: millivolts; m/s: meters/second, (s): sensory, (m): motor

EMG

Left	Spontaneous activity	Motor unit potentials	Recruitment
Deltoid	N	N	N
Triceps	N	N	N
Extensor carpi radialis (LH)	Increased	N/Abnormal	N/Reduced
Brachioradialis	Increased	N/Abnormal	N/Reduced
Extensor digitorum communis	Increased	N/Abnormal	N/Reduced
Extensor carpi ulnaris	Increased	N/Abnormal	N/Reduced
Extensor indicis	Increased	Abnormal	Reduced
Pronator teres	N	N	N
1st dorsal interosseous	N	N	N
Abductor pollicis brevis	N	N	N
Cervical paraspinals	N	N	N
Right			
Extensor indicis	N	N	N

N: normal, LH: long head

In summary, you concur this is a left radial sensorimotor neuropathy with conduction block across the spiral groove and features of sensory and motor demyelination and axon loss. There is active/evolving denervation with changes in motor unit configuration and recruitment patterns in the distribution of the radial/posterior interosseous nerves. Reduced recruitment is a common finding with conduction block.

3. What would you recommend for a comprehensive rehabilitation program?

The patient would benefit from a referral to occupational therapy (A/PROM, strengthening, nerve glides, HEP) and perhaps wrist splinting to help restore function. Adaptive equipment should also be considered for activities of daily living. Splinting may be static, dynamic, or combination with goal to maintain range of motion, prevent contractures of hand/wrist joints, and assist with function during recovery. Close follow-up is needed to assess improvement.

4. The patient returns to your office 2-months later and was doing well until he was involved in a motorcycle accident and fractured his arm in the same place and had to undergo open reduction internal fixation. He now has 0/5 strength of wrist and finger extension. You send him for another EMG and this time there is concern for neurotmesis of the radial nerve. What do you do?

Prognosis is poor in this type of nerve injury. A referral to an orthopedic surgeon for surgical evaluation is necessary.

5. He asks you why last time he had full recovery with rehabilitation and this time you are sending him to a surgeon?

Engage the patient and acknowledge the great question. Explain to the patient in lay terms about the different types of nerve injuries with use of visuals if possible. Tell him that this time it appears the nerve has been transected and is no longer delivering signals to the muscles. This often requires surgery. In some situations, you tell him, nerves do regrow but at a very slow rate and completeness of reinnervation is dependent on several factors including distance from the muscle and structures it must grow through which has an influence on prognosis. With his case, you feel he will have the best chance of recovering function if he has surgical exploration and repair. You assure him you will follow his progress and will be involved in his post-operative rehabilitation. Be positive in outlook, without diminishing the challenges. You tell him you are available for questions anytime.

Note: Educating patients on prognosis is very important. For cases of nerve injury, outcome depends on type of nerve injury:

- **Neuropraxia**: normal function is usually regained in 2-8 weeks (can be up to 6 months). Recovery is by remyelination.
- **Axonotmesis**: recovery will generally take longer, but recovery is usually very good. Recovery is by regrowth (~1mm/day) or collateral sprouting.
- **Neurotmesis**: with discontinuity of the axon and surrounding connective tissue there is poor recovery, even with surgical repair.

References:

Preston D and Shapiro B. Electromyography and neuromuscular disorders, 2nd edition. 1998;327-342.

Nguyen G. Radial nerve mononueruopathy. PM&R Knowledge now. Last updated July 2021. https://now.aapmr.org.

Asif I, Mangan J and Graham J. Radial nerve palsy recovery with fractures of the humerus: an updated systematic review. J AAOS. 2020;28(60):e2630e269.

Case: Cervical dystonia

A 64-year-old male presents to your outpatient clinic as a referral from primary care to be evaluated for botulinum neurotoxin injections for cervical dystonia ("spasmodic torticollis").

1. What additional information about his history and examination would you like to know?

Patient was diagnosed with cervical dystonia (CD) 20 years ago by his neurologist who just retired. He has no family history and was told it was idiopathic. He was receiving botulinum toxin injections every 3-4 months that reduced his pain significantly. His pain is otherwise severe with radiation to the side of head deviation. If he doesn't have the injections, it is difficult for him to work in his cabinetry business. He is otherwise healthy, eats a well-balanced diet, and exercises regularly. On examination, the left sternocleidomastoid (SCM) has modified Asworth Scale (MAS) of 3. There are no sensory or motor deficits of the cranial nerves, upper or lower limbs. Reflexes are normal in the upper and lower limbs. Babinski and Hoffman's are negative.

2. Is there indication for additional work up?

Yes, pain is the mainstay of this disorder. However, there are secondary orthopedic conditions that could be contributing as a pain source such as spondylosis, disc herniation, fracture, radiculopathy, myofascial pain, and myelopathy – and should be excluded. X-rays and advanced imaging could be helpful, and selection of the best test/radiology should be guided clinically.

3. What is your management plan for this patient?

Ordering x-rays of the neck for evaluation of orthopedic conditions would be prudent prior to initiating botulinum neurotoxin injections. The x-rays showed moderate degenerative disc disease throughout the cervical spine with mild facet arthropathy. You are comfortable with the diagnosis of focal cervical dystonia given the radiographic findings do not correlate with the clinical presentation. Your received insurance authorization so you give the patient botulinum neurotoxin injection to the SCM. You schedule a 6-week phone call follow-up to check efficacy. A referral to physical therapy for re-education of movement patterns, HEP, ROM/stretching, antagonist muscle strengthening, sensory disinhibition, proprioception, and modalities (FES) may be considered. Stress can worsen the intensity of symptoms and thus management of stress and/or depression is important. Referrals to psychology/psychiatry should be considered.

4. Patient is doing well at 6-week follow up and asks about the pros/cons of the other spasticity injections. He has a friend who gets something different. How do you reply?

You can review other medications that would yield similar results. Inform the patient that medications are often chosen based on the need of the patient. Since the Botox injections are working well, you would recommend continuing for now. However, let him now that these other options will be explored if he loses benefit with botulinum neurotoxin.

Available botulinum toxins for treatment of cervical dystonia

Agent	Trade name	Notes
Onabotulnum toxin A	Botox	Common 1st line; can develop antibody resistance
Abobotulinum toxin B	Dysport	Greater spread may lead to more diffuse distribution
Incobotulinum toxin A	Xeomin	No complexing proteins which may have greater efficacy and less risk of antibody formation or sensitization
Rimabotulinum toxin B	Myobloc	Acidic pH can cause injection discomfort Can reduce sialorrhea

5. The patient missed his last injection and is in severe pain. His wife calls and asks if he can get in to see you today. Your clinic is already double-booked. How would you respond?

Use active listening and compassionate responses. Explore reasons and/or barriers that led to missing the last appointment. Discuss with the patient and his wife that you understand the pain is severe and you will see what you can do to get him seen urgently. The patient and his wife thank you for being understanding of the situation and appreciate the appointment. Remember, patient centered care and a timely response are essential.

Notes: Chemical denervation with Botox (or other agents) should be tailored to the individual and should start at a lowered dose and adjusted based on individual response. Clinical improvement generally begins within 2-3 weeks after the injection, with peak effect around 6 weeks, and return to pretreatment status by 3 months. Ultrasound or EMG are commonly used for procedural accuracy.

The Toronto Western Spasmodic Torticollis Rating Scale (TWSTRS) was developed as an assessment scale used to measure the impact of CD on patients by measuring severity, disability, and pain.

Measurement of spasticity is commonly with use of the standardized Modified Ashworth Scale.

Modified Ashworth Scale:

0: No increase in muscle tone

1: Slight increase in muscle tone, with a catch and release or minimal resistance at the end of the range of motion when an affected part(s) is moved in flexion or extension

1+: Slight increase in muscle tone, manifested as a catch, followed by minimal resistance through the remainder (less than half) of the range of motion

2: A marked increase in muscle tone throughout most of the range of motion, but affected part(s) are still easily moved

3: Considerable increase in muscle tone, passive movement difficult

4: Affected part(s) rigid in flexion or extension

Resources:

Farzal Z, Lamotte G, Mundel E, Bahroo L, and Pagan L. Movement disorders moment: treatment approaches to cervical dystonia. Practical neurology. Oct 2020. https://praticalneurology.com.

Ferreira JJ, Costa J, Coelho M, and Sampaio C. The management of cervical dystonia. Expert Opin Pharmacother. 2007 Feb;8(2):129-40. doi: 10.1517/14656566.8.2.129. PMID: 17257084.

Jost W, Hefter H, Stenner A, and Reichel G. Rating scales for cervical dystonia: a critical evalatuion of tools for outcome assessment of botulinum toxin therapy. J Neural Transm (Vienna). 2013; 120(3): 487–496. 2012 Aug 17. doi: 10.1007/s00702-012-0887-7.

Meseguer-Henarejos AB, Sánchez-Meca J, López-Pina JA, and Carles-Hernández R. Inter- and intra-rater reliability of the Modified Ashworth Scale: a systematic review and meta-analysis. Eur J Phys Rehabil Med. 2018 Aug;54(4):576-590.

Case: Weakness

A 21-year-old male who has been hospitalized for lower limb weakness and shortness of breath.

1. What would you like to know on history and physical examination?

He was admitted to the hospital 2-days ago with a 1-week history of ascending leg weakness and paresthesia. He had been sick with the flu about 2-weeks ago. His current symptoms are described as numbness and tingling in the legs and fingertips. He has shortness of breath but is not requiring respiratory support or supplemental oxygen. Review of systems is negative for history of back pain, vision changes, and bowel/bladder changes. Neurology has initiated IVIg therapy for an immunologic demyelinating condition. He has not noticed improvement yet, but he has gotten out of bed with physical therapy requiring moderate assistance. Prior, he was independent with mobility and self-cares as baseline. On focused physical examination he is alert and oriented to person, place, time, and situation. He has absent Achilles and patellar reflexes with loss of sensation in the lower legs, feet, and hands. He has weakness, 3/5 distally, and 3+/5 proximally in the lower limbs, and 4/5 in the upper limbs distally. Tone is normal. Cranial nerves are normal. Vital signs are stable.

2. What is a comprehensive differential in ascending paresthesia and weakness? What would an early EMG look like?

This patient has acute inflammatory demyelinating polyradiculopathy, "Guillain-Barre Syndrome" (GBS). Your differential may also include compressive myelopathy, disc herniation, transverse myelitis, chronic inflammatory demyelinating neuropathy (CIDP), HIV-related radiculitis, Lyme disease, leptomeningeal malignancy, toxic neuropathy, vasculitis, botulism, multiple sclerosis, myasthenia gravis, periodic paralysis, and hereditary spastic paraparesis.

You reviewed the chart and saw the inpatient EMG had characteristic early GBS findings of prolonged F-waves, absent H-waves, borderline abnormal sensory nerve action potentials (SNAPs), and preserved sural responses. Conduction blocks were not seen in the motor studies, but you know this may be a later electrodiagnostic feature. The lumbar paraspinals and many upper and lower limb muscles had abnormal spontaneous activity and reduced recruitment.

3. As a consultant, you recommend admission to inpatient rehabilitation. What is your comprehensive rehabilitation plan?

A comprehensive program involving physical and occupational therapy with focus on progressive resistive exercises, range of motion, strengthening, proper limb positioning, postural training, gait training, adaptive equipment, and durable medical equipment. Ankle foot orthotics may also be considered with his focal weakness in the lower limbs. Social work services can assist the patient with psychosocial issues, for example, addressing various housing, occupational and/or scholastic problems that may arise. Discharge planning may also include setting up patient for vocational rehab. Chaplain services may help patients spiritually fostering a whole person care model. Patients experiencing sudden loss of function, or catastrophic illness, are facing uncertainly and would likely benefit from intensive psychology/psychiatry for coping and adjustment. Nutrition should be optimized. Patients may ask about community support groups, or you can suggest it! Monitor patient for complications such as deep venous thrombosis, pain management, wound care, and bowel/bladder management. The physiatrist should incorporate education about the condition and update prognosis throughout the rehab stay.

4. What type of mobility device would you recommend for him? What would your wheelchair prescription include?

The most appropriate device is selected based on the patient's ability and prognosis. The patient improved 1 muscle grade over the course of acute rehab, except in the distal lower limbs with residual weakness, 3/5. He is easily fatigued and requires frequent rest breaks. You recommend a 4-wheeled walker for shorter distances (with AFO's) and a wheelchair for community.

The components of the wheelchair could be light or ultralight weight, with the latter popular for sports. You may add features of detachable or swing away footrests, height adjustable arms, and custom seating. Power mobility would not be appropriate in this case.

5. Your patient comes to your office as a post hospital discharge visit 3 weeks later. He is extremely depressed. He used to play basketball and he thinks he will never play again. What do you tell him?

Express compassion and acknowledge the patient's feelings. Without diminishing how he feels, provide hope and reassurance. Ask the patient about his support system. Ask him about thoughts of danger to self or others.

Discuss with him about some options for para-sporting activities, including basketball, and give him resources to investigate. Encourage him to stay engaged in work, school, and sports and offer your assistance for accommodations/paperwork needed with respect to each. Offer him a referral for ongoing outpatient psychology/psychiatry visits and schedule regular follow up.

Notes: Wheelchair (WC) prescriptions are based in part, on the individual's functional ability (i.e., strength, ROM, head and trunk control), activity level (sedentary, athlete), home set-up, skin integrity, intended use/terrain, portability, and disease prognosis (improving, static, or progressive). For example, for post-operative patients who typically have a self-limited condition, a standard WC would be sufficient for most. Others may need customized WCs with special features such as tilt-in-space, reclining seat back, high-back trunk support, and/or head rest (i.e., SCI, ALS). Seating systems are customizable and help reduce pressure wounds. There are also wheelchairs customizable for adaptive sports aimed at performance.

Wheelchair Type	Weight
Standard	40-65 lb
Lightweight	30-35 lb
Ultralightweight (aluminum)	<30 lb
Ultralightweight (titanium)	<20 lb

References:

Gordon P and Wilbourn A. Early electrodiagnostic findings in Guillain-Barre syndrome. Arch Neurol. 2001 Jun;58(6):913-7. doi 10.1001/archneur.58.6.913.

Meythaler J. Rehabilitation of Guillain-Barre syndrome. Arch Phys med. 1997 Aug;78(8):872-879. doi 10.1016/50003-999(97)90203-3.

Khan F, Ng L, Amatya B, Brand C, and Turner-Stokes L. Multidisciplinary care for Guillain-Barre syndrome. Cochrane Database of Systematic Reviews. https://doi.org/10.1002/14651858.CD008505.pub2.

Baby M, O-Reilly, Jackson K, Gadgil R, and Patro A. Wheelchair prescription. https://www.physio-pedia.com/Wheelchair_Prescription.

Case: Mid-Back Pain

A 79-year-old male presents to your outpatient musculoskeletal clinic with severe back pain for the last 4-weeks.

1. What would you like to know about his history and physical examination?

He has multiple co-morbidities, including hypertension, diabetes, "elevated PSA", and COPD with a 50-year history of smoking. He lives with his wife in a singlewide mobile home. He uses a front wheeled walker for household distances and power mobility in the community. Over the last year he notes unintentional weight loss of 30 pounds. He has nocturnal awakenings with night sweats and intermittent low-grade fevers. He is also having difficulty urinating with hematuria. His pain is "10/10" and radiates up and down the mid-back region. He is taking opioids prescribed by his primary care doctor with no relief. He has fallen several times in his home because of tripping with resultant abrasions on his arms and legs. He thinks his new weakness is because of the pain the is further elucidated as "lancinating pain." On examination, he winces occasionally with pain. He appears thin, with good hygiene, and is a good historian. He has bruises on his arms and legs at various stages of healing. Cranial nerves are intact. He has mid-line and paraspinal tenderness at T8-T12. He has impaired sensation circumferentially bilaterally up to knees, and on bilateral hands to wrist. His motor examination is non-focal, 4/5 in the in the lower limbs and full strength in the upper limbs. His reflexes are normal. Tone is normal. Babinski's, Hoffman's, and Palmomental are negative. He has a sensory type ("stomping") gait and fair balance and takes frequent rest breaks. His vital signs are stable, and he is afebrile.

2. What is your differential diagnosis and what would your work-up be?

This patient has a concerning history for cancer with unintentional weight loss, night sweats, history of elevated PSA, and smoking. Another high possibility is fracture(s) considering the recurrent falls; he has risk for both pathologic and traumatic etiologies of back pain. Other considerations are thoracic or lumbosacral central stenosis, spondylosis, spondylolisthesis, radiculopathy/polyradiculopathy, discitis/osteomyelitis, transverse myelitis, compression fracture(s), tumor (primary or metastatic), spine cysts, or vascular (watershed infarct, aneurysm). Concomitantly, diabetic polyneuropathy ("stocking glove") would be suspected.

Since he will not go to ER, you decide to admit him to your acute rehab unit for work-up, pain management, and rehabilitation. You get x-rays of the thoracic and lumbar spines with multilevel degenerative disc disease with evidence of acute burst fracture at T10 and remote compression fractures at L2 and L3. Initial labs will include CBC with differential, CMP, PSA (prostate cancer), ESR, CRP and perhaps SPEP/UPEP (multiple myeloma), and lactate dehydrogenase (LDH) (lymphoma/leukemia).

His PSA is markedly abnormal, 20 ng/mL (normal 0-6.5 ng/mL for age) and you consult urology for possible prostate cancer, and learn it was previously confirmed by biopsy, but patient did not seek treatment. Advanced imaging may include CT (abdomen and pelvis) and a bone scan and/or PET scan to evaluate metastatic lesions. DEXA scan should be considered in patients with history of compression fractures or osteopenia on x-ray. In this case, MRI or CT (+/- myelogram) of the thoracic spine can delineate spinal cord or nerve root compression from the T10 pathologic burst fracture. You see no mass effect on the spinal cord or nerve roots on his scans. You consult orthopedics (or neurosurgery) for spinal stabilization, and they agree to take him to the OR after preop medical clearance. Note, if the patient is not a surgical candidate, bracing (i.e., TLSO) or body casting may be recommended by the surgical service.

3. The patient returns to your service status post T9-T11 decompression and fusion. What is your comprehensive rehabilitation plan for this patient? What special considerations would you have about precautions?

A multidisciplinary approach will include surgical wound care, bowel and bladder management, pain management, therapies (physical therapy, occupational therapy), social work, psychology, chaplain, and discharge planner. Consultation with urology and oncology to develop a plan for his prostate cancer treatment and for cancer staging. Other considerations, spinal precautions and TLSO bracing while out of bed >30 degrees are standard practice for this type of spine surgery and compliance needs to be monitored. Along with medical management of co-morbidities, this patient is at risk for developing deep venous thrombosis (post-op, cancer hypercoagulability, falls/trauma, smoking) and chemical prophylaxis or sequential compression devices (SCD's) should be initiated. Referral to preventative medicine or one-to-one discussion about the benefits of smoking cessation would be timely.

4. Your patient makes an appointment 1-year later after being lost to follow up. He had chemotherapy and radiation and is in remission. He has concerns about urinary incontinence and "numbness and tingling in the feet." What is your guidance?

In terms of the urinary incontinence, you review the chart and see urology has ruled out organic causes (i.e., benign prostate hypertrophy, overactive bladder, cancer recurrence) and he has no findings on history and exam of central nervous system causes. You decide to send the patient for pelvic floor therapy (Kegel exercises).

Regarding his numbness and tingling, you appreciate his history of diabetes and suspect he has a component of diabetic neuropathy. However, he may also have neuropathy related to the chemotherapeutic agents. To further characterize the neuropathy, you may refer him for NCS/EMG. You may also consider neuropathic or topical agents for analgesia (caution with sedating medications that can increase fall risk). Outpatient physical therapy for assistive device evaluation, gait mechanics, neuromuscular retraining, and proprioception could be recommended if he is still experiencing falls and balance issues.

5. At the next visit the patient is upset because he never got scheduled for pelvic floor therapy. What will you tell him?

You: "I am so sorry to learn that you were not able to schedule your therapy Mr. Jones. Let me make a few calls and see what I can do to get this lined out for you. I am going to step out briefly to get this taken care of. May I offer you something to drink while you are waiting?" Mr. Jones: "No. just get my therapy! This incontinence is embarrassing." You: "Ok, I understand. I will be right back." You discover the therapy order was never sent and has now expired. You return to the room. You: "Mr. Jones, I want to let you know that it was our mistake. It looks like the therapy order was never sent. I just wrote another order and called the facility to expedite scheduling. They have an appointment for you this week. I am sorry about this delay and duress it has caused. I will call you later this week to see how your first visit goes." Mr. Jones, "Well, I figured something like this happened. I do appreciate your honesty. Thank you for helping me get an appointment this week." Acknowledging the mistake followed by corrective action is the right thing to do, ethically and professionally.

References:

Price N, Dawood R, and Jackson S. Pelvic floor exercise for urinary incontinence: A systematic literature review. Maturitas. 2010;67(4):p309-315. ISSN 0378-5122. https://doi.org/10.1016/j.maturitas.2010.08.004.

Kim NH, Lee HM, and Chun IM. Neurologic injury and recovery in patients with burst fracture of the thoracolumbar spine. Spine. February 1999;24(3):p290-293.

Kato S, Murray JC. Kwon BK, Schroeder GD, Vaccaro AR, and Fehlings, MG. Does surgical intervention or timing of surgery have an effect on neurological recovery in the setting of a thoracolumbar burst fracture? Journal of Orthopaedic Trauma: September 2017;31: p S38-S43 doi: 10.1097/BOT.0000000000000946.

Litwin MS and Tan H. The Diagnosis and Treatment of Prostate Cancer: A review. *JAMA*. 2017;317(24):2532–2542. doi:10.1001/jama.2017.7248.

Huang ME and Sliwa JA. Inpatient Rehabilitation of Patients with Cancer: Efficacy and Treatment Considerations. PM&R. 2011;3:p746-757. https://doi.org/10.1016/j.pmrj.2011.05.020.

Vargo, M, Clark M, Khanna A, and Christensen Holz S. Cancer Rehabilitation Medical Knowledge for Physiatry Residents: Literature Subtopic Analysis and Synthesis into Key Domains. Journal of Injury, Function and Rehabilitation. 2020;12:p829-836. https://doi.org/10.1002/pmrj.12314.

Case: Neck Pain

A 62-year-old former alpine skiing Olympian presents to your office via telehealth with a 2-year history of neck pain and "clumsy hands and legs".

1.For this *virtual visit*, what would you like to know on history and physical examination?

She has no medical co-morbidities and has had neck pain off and on for 10 years of insidious onset but noticeably worsening pain and function. She used to be an avid skier even after her Olympic years and has sustained skiing accidents of varying severity with none involving her neck. Her neck pain is "achy", and she has noticed loss of manual dexterity in her hands, weakness, stiffness, and balance issues. She gives a description of numbness as, "it feels like I have gloves on my hands". She uses holistic supplements for pain control and has not seen a doctor for this before. On review of symptoms, she has occasional urinary incontinence and poor coordination, no bowel changes, no weight loss, and no vision changes. Functionally, she has borrowed a friend's walker who insisted she use it after too many falls. She lives alone in a 2-story home in an isolated community in the mountains. On video examination, she has limited cervical range of motion due to guarding, she makes a facial grimace induced by the effort of trying to raise her arms overhead. She shows you her hands to outline the area of numbness (up to bilateral forearms) and you notice she has intrinsic hand atrophy. When she stands, she holds onto the desk for stabilization. She grabs her walker, and you notice her gait is spastic (be sure to have her use the walker and scan the room for safety hazards – especially with history of falls and balance impairment. If possible, see if someone is home to supervise or defer gait assessment if unsafe.)

2. What is the differential diagnosis? What is the next step for evaluation?

You suspect cervical myelopathy. Other considerations would be ALS though less likely given her sensory symptoms (motor neuron disease "painless weakness"), GBS with predominant distal weakness and sensory changes, CIDP, normal pressure hydrocephalus ("wacky"/cognitive changes, "wobbly"/balance impairment, "wet"/urinary incontinence), brainstem or intracranial lesion, cervical radiculopathy, spondylosis, and multiple sclerosis.

You schedule her for an urgent office visit the next day. On examination, she has weakness, 4/5 diffusely. Sensation is diminished to pinprick in the hands up to mid-forearm and in the feet and trunk. Her reflexes are 3+ biceps, triceps, patellar, Achilles and she has a positive crossed adductor sign, jaw jerk is negative. Babinski's and Hoffman's are positive and palmomental is negative. Tone is increased in her legs and arms with 1+ modified Ashworth. She has several beats of clonus bilaterally. Her gait is spastic.

3. What is your work up?

You order x rays that shows multilevel degenerative changes, severe in degree. You get a stat MRI and is shows severe cervical stenosis with myelomalacia (high signal changes with T2-weighted MRI). There is ligamentum flavum hypertrophy and disc bulges that combine to cause central stenosis. If there is a contraindication to MRI, CT with or without myelogram can be ordered. You recommend consultation with neurosurgery or orthopedic spine. With these findings you recommend a hard collar (i.e., aspen collar) to minimize cervical movement.

4. The patient is not convinced she needs surgery and asks about conservative treatment. Specifically, she would like a soft cervical support brace and a referral to see a chiropractor and acupuncturist. What are the concerns and contraindications?

Chiropractic manipulation can cause paralysis in this patient with neurologic compromise, especially if high-velocity manipulation is sought. It is an absolute contra-indication, and this patient should not be given a referral. Acupuncture is a complementary and alternative medicine (CAM) option for palliative pain control; however, it should not be used in-lieu of surgical evaluation. Delaying surgical intervention can lead to paralysis.

A soft collar should not be used as it is not supportive enough. These types of collars are sometimes used for comfort in patients with neck pain. This patient would need a hard collar.

With evidence of myelomalacia, this patient will need a referral to a SCI specialist following surgery. Occupational therapy for dexterity, fine motor control, and coordination. Physical therapy for balance, gait and strengthening. Pain management (spasms, spasticity) will also be important.

5. She tells you she is too afraid to have surgery and is going to cancel. What would you tell her?

Utilize nonverbal strategies such as sitting down and make eye contact. Ask the patient about her specific fears and help her reconcile them with medical facts and compassion. Sometimes patients are fearful because of the unknown, give her a roadmap of the process. Be supportive, not dismissive. You: "Ms. Summit, I am hearing you are very worried. I can understand how this can be overwhelming and really scary. Tell me more." Use open ended questions, active listening, and reassurance. Ms. Summit: "I live alone, and what if I need help to go home? I don't want to live at a SNF." You explain the typical transition of care for rehabilitation at hospital discharge, and if she were to go to a SNF, you tell her it is usually short-term during recovery. Start talking about the possibility of caregiver support services and explore friends/family who can help her at home (they will need family training). Ms. Summit: "Oh, thank you. I feel better now. I'll have the surgery.

Notes: Remember, with video visits, getting location of the patient during the visit and their emergency contact is essential in case they have a medical emergency during the virtual visit.

You can perform a virtual "physical examination" by having the patient be task-oriented. For example, stand on your tip toes (S1) and heels (L4/5), touch your toes (neural tension signs), make a fist and release repeatedly (coordination). Always default to the safest examinations that will yield the most information and defer if the examination is not safe for the patient to perform by themselves.

References:

Bakhsheshian J, Mehta V, and Liu J. Current diagnosis and management of cervical sponydlytic myelopathy. Global Spine J. 2017 Sep;7(6):572-586. PMID: 28894688. doiI: 10.1177/2192568217699208.

Laskowsk E, et al. The telemedicine musculoskeletal examination. Mayo Clinic Proceedings. 2020;95:1715.

Emery S. Cervical Spondylotic Myelopathy: Diagnosis and Treatment. J of the American Academy of Orthopaedic Surgeons: November 2001;9(6):p376-388 doi: 10.1097/BRS.0b013e3182a7f449.

Harrop JS, Naroji, S, Maltenfort M, Anderson D, Albert T, Ratliff JK, Ponnappan Ravi K, Smith J, Hilibrand A, Sharan A, Vaccaro A. Cervical Myelopathy. Spine. March 2010;35(6):p620-624 doi: 10.1097/BRS.0b013e3181b723af.

Case: Breast Cancer with lymphedema

A 40-year-old female with history of breast cancer status-post left mastectomy presents to your office for rehabilitation and lymphedema management.

1. What would you like to know for her history and physical examination?

She was diagnosed with breast cancer 5 years ago. She had a family history (maternal) of breast cancer and genetic testing showed BRCA 1 and 2 mutations. She went for a mammogram and a mass was detected, biopsied, and returned a cancer diagnosis. She had a mastectomy with lymph node resection, followed by chemotherapy (i.e., taxans (taxol), 5-fluorouracil (5-FU)) and radiation therapy. She has numbness in her feet and fingertips due to the chemotherapy. She uses a compression sleeve for lymphedema management and daily HEP for range of motion of the left arm and shoulder. She has intermittent swelling of the left arm with "heaviness" during episodes. She is a CEO of a local grocery chain and works 6 days a week as a self-described "workaholic". The review of systems is negative for shoulder or neck pain. On examination, skin has normal turgor and no discoloration or fibrotic changes. She has minimally decreased left shoulder and neck range of motion, no motor deficits, and intact reflexes. Sensation is diminished distally in the upper and lower limbs. Gait is normal.

2. What are some causes and risk factors for lymphedema? If cause is uncertain, what tests would you choose?

1) Cancer is a common cause with tumor growth or cancer cells causing blockage of the lymphatic system. 2) Radiation treatment for cancer can cause scarring or inflammation of

the lymph nodes and vessels. 3) Surgery to resect lymph nodes can sometimes be a cause. 4) Most common in developing countries, parasites that invade and block the lymphatic system.

Risk factors include history of cancer, older age, obesity, and rheumatoid conditions. Cellulitis is a common complication.

MRI, CT, Ultrasound and Lymphoscintography can all evaluate lymphatic flow or blockage.

3.What is an outpatient rehabilitation plan for this patient? What type of education can you give to reduce occurrence?

Referral to a lymphedema specialist for wrapping and retrograde massage. Physical therapy for ROM (shoulder, cervical), strengthening, and HEP. Modalities will be limited due to history of cancer. Elevation of the affected limb can help with gravity assisted drainage. If the patient has depression, refer to psychology/psychiatry. Involvement in support groups and community fundraising events can be empowering and socially pleasing.

To protect the affected limb, you suggest the patient avoid venipuncture or injections in that arm, blood pressure cuffs on the arm, tight bands or clothing, carry handbags and heavy packages on the opposite side, prevent sun burns, clean the skin daily with gentle soap and lotion, low sodium diet, avoid extremes in temperature (hot/cold), avoid scrubbing the skin, and treat signs/symptoms of infection aggressively.

4.What are some components of an outpatient cancer rehabilitation program?

Patients may have cancer-related or cancer-treatment-related problems. The overall aim is to help them maintain and restore physical and emotional well-being before, during, or after cancer treatment. Overarching areas: Performance/function (physical, cognitive, exercise, mobility, fatigue), treatment and effects (surgery, chemotherapy, radiation, neurologic), bone mets and bone health (spine mets, long bone mets, osteopenia/osteoporosis), and lymphedema. Multidisciplinary teams typically include PT (endurance, strength, and mobility), OT (activities of daily living/instrumental activities of daily living), mental health (build confidence and self-esteem, coping with anxiety and/or distress, depression), and a physiatrist. Formulation of long-term plan for cancer survivorship is a cornerstone. Other services include medical and/or surgical oncology and palliative or end-of-life care.

A cancer rehab specialist will oversee a patient's rehabilitation, spasticity management, prosthetic prescription for amputees, performs NCS/EMG, work up functional decline (H&P, imaging, labs), and pain management. The physiatrist works closely with hematology/oncology, radiation oncology, surgical oncology, and palliative care for care coordination.

5.She was recently treated for cellulitis with a 10-day course of antibiotics. She was given antibiotics that she had an allergy to and suggests she is going to sue the doctor but wants to know what you think.

You ask her what type of allergic reaction she had and check the chart to see if she has a listed allergy. She had an anaphylactic reaction, and the allergy was added in the ED. You explain to her that sometimes people have unknown allergies to certain medications, and it is hard to predict. You tell her you are happy that she was able to get treated urgently and she is feeling better. You do not affirm her suggestion that someone "did something wrong" rather, you remain nonjudgmental and unaccusatory in your explanation and tone. She appreciates the explanation and now understands how it could happen without fault to anyone.

References:

Silver JK and Gilchrist LS. Cancer rehabilitation with a focus on evidence-based outpatient physical and occupational therapy interventions. Am J Phys Med Rehabil. 2011 May;90(5 Suppl 1):S5-15. doi: 10.1097/PHM.0b013e31820be4ae. PMID: 21765263.

Armer JM, Hulett JM, Bernas M, et al. Best-Practice Guidelines in Assessment, Risk Reduction, Management, and Surveillance for Post-Breast Cancer Lymphedema. Curr Breast Cancer Rep. 2013;5:134–144. https://doi.org/10.1007/s12609-013-0105-0.

Doscher ME, Schreiber JE, Weichman KE, and Garfein, E.S. (2016), Update on Post-mastectomy Lymphedema Management. Breast J, 22: 553-560. https://doi.org/10.1111/tbj.12625.

AFTERWORD

In the wise words of the Hitchhiker's Guide to the Galaxy, "Don't Panic!" When in doubt, the answer is not 42. It is "I would do a team-based approach." Remember you are a highly intelligent and competent human being. Talk yourself up. Practice hard.

ABOUT THE AUTHORS

The authors are experienced practitioners, teachers, parents, siblings, children, and all around good people. They put a lot of work into this book and training residents over the years. One of the authors made pretend magic physiatric-imbued chocolates to eat before the test. One of the author's family moved her out of the house before the test because of her study habits. Just remember, however stressed you are, you probably have not made magic chocolates or have been moved out of the house. Now, go rock that test!

www.ingramcontent.com/pod-product-compliance
Lightning Source LLC
Chambersburg PA
CBHW070638300426
44111CB00013B/2157